Scribe Publications
ARABIAN PLIGHTS

Peter Rodgers is a former Australian ambassador to Israel, and is a regular commentator on Middle Eastern affairs. He is also the author of *Herzl's Nightmare*, and a former journalist and winner of the Graham Perkin Australian Journalist of the Year Award for his reporting on East Timor.

For my brothers and sister

ARABIAN PLIGHTS

the future Middle East

Peter Rodgers

SCRIBE
Melbourne

Scribe Publications Pty Ltd
PO Box 523
Carlton North, Victoria, Australia 3054
Email: info@scribepub.com.au

First published by Scribe 2009

Typeset in 11.75/16.5 pt Bembo by the publishers
Printed and bound in Australia by Griffin Press
Only wood grown from sustainable regrowth forests is used in the
manufacture of paper found in this book.

National Library of Australia
Cataloguing-in-Publication data

Rodgers, Peter.
Arabian plights: the future Middle East

9781921215285 (pbk.)

Arab-Israeli conflict; Jewish-Arab relations; Peace–Religious aspects;
Peace-building–Middle East; Peaceful change (International relations)–
21st century; Reconciliation–Palestine; Palestine–Foreign relations–
Israel.

956.94

www.scribepublications.com.au

Contents

Introduction

In 1984, *The Economist* magazine decided to predict the future. It asked select groups of finance ministers, senior businessmen, and Oxford university students for their vision of the world, economically, ten years down the track. In 1994, the groups' written responses were unsealed and checked against the realities. As soothsayers, each group performed dismally, being either wildly optimistic or needlessly pessimistic. Overall, the businessmen performed best—but no more accurately than the London garbage-men recruited as the 'control' for the project.

That each group got it wrong should hardly surprise. Churchill reputedly once advised that prophesying is best done after the event. But even then, even after the 'future' has become the 'past' and we have the 'facts' before us, we still argue about what happened, and why, and what it meant. Who at the beginning of the twentieth century could have imagined the dramatic changes that were to occur over the next hundred years: the extraordinary advances in medicine, the transformation of human communication, the unleashing of previously unthinkable destructive power, and the devastating effects of great wars that changed forever the geographic and social map of the world? Think, too, of the shocks and surprises on the world stage in just the past few decades: the emergence of AIDS as a danger to individual health and the very existence of some African and other nation states; the collapse of the Soviet Union and the end of the communist ideal as a force in world affairs; the 2001 attacks on the World Trade Center and other symbols of American power; and the rise of the terrorist threat in Western consciousness, even though the reality of 'terrorism' is as old as humankind. To these, mostly unforeseen, developments we should add terrible natural events worldwide — earthquakes and hurricanes, floods and fires — consuming countless lives and livelihoods. And all this is happening in a world where our capacity to understand our planet and interact with each other is constantly re-inventing itself.

Our knowledge of the past is often a poor guide to the future even if, realistically, it is all we have. The limitations on charting the future might seem a good argument for leaving it well alone. Yet as long as humans have been around, they have pondered the shape of tomorrow's world. Much of this may be little more than idle curiosity. But, often, it will have a pragmatic end. Many personal, corporate, and state decisions are based on what might happen in six months, two years, or 30 years hence. The scout's motto, 'be prepared', still has a lot to recommend it.

This book sets out to glimpse the future Middle East. The rationale for this is straightforward. Of all the world's regions, none outranks the Middle East in how it will continue to impact on our daily lives — overtly and covertly. As long as the world runs on oil, it will run on the Middle East. Consider this: some 90 per cent of the world's transportation — whether by land or sea or air — needs oil. Some 95 per cent of all the food we eat uses oil in some way. And 90 per cent of all the products in our shops require the use of oil, either directly or indirectly. Consider, also, that the Middle East holds at least two-thirds of the world's known oil reserves (more if we include Iran, often viewed as part of the broader Middle East). After Middle Eastern nations and Venezuela, the next-largest oil reserves are in Russia — home also of the world's largest natural gas reserves — a country which has shown, in no uncertain terms, that it will use this bounty for strategic advantage.

Despite our flirtations with alternative forms of energy — with solar, wind, wave, and nuclear power — and despite dire warnings to mend our ways and reduce our dependence on a few, exotic Middle Eastern states, we are all oil junkies. Can we really see America reducing its oil imports from the Middle East by 75 per cent in just 20 years, as the second president

Bush once envisaged? Middle Eastern states know that we are hooked and that we will stay this way. If the predictions of the International Energy Agency (IEA) are any guide, over the next quarter-century we will become more, not less, dependent on Middle Eastern oil. And, providing substantial investment is forthcoming, oil and gas revenues in that region will more than double from their present levels to a staggering $635 billion a year. (All dollar figures are US unless indicated otherwise.)

Like many addicts, we resent our dealer. We can't or won't change ourselves in any dramatic fashion, but we want Middle Eastern states to do so. The early years of the 21st century saw a sharpening global focus on the nature of Arab politics. The extraordinary terrorist attacks on American soil in September 2001 drove the US-led war against the Taliban regime in Afghanistan, and added a dubious rationale for the later overthrow of Iraq's Saddam Hussein. Partly as a consequence of this, debate intensified about what the Arab world stood for, its stress points, and its often sclerotic governance. Leaving aside the running sore of Israel and Palestine, are the problems of the Middle East peculiarly Islamic, peculiarly Arab, or a peculiarly unsavoury combination of the two? Is Arab society, with its strongly entrenched tribal traditions and etiquettes, more resistant to change than those countries or regions in which old traditions have significantly decayed?

It is wrong, of course, to speak of the Middle East or the Arab world as though it is a tightly knit homogenous entity. A common language and a sense of shared traditions, especially Islam, underpins its self-identification. But it is a mistake to view all Arabs as fervently religious, or even Islamic. The region, like many others, has its share of communal and religious fracture, with Arabs, Kurds, Berbers, Sunni Muslims, Shia Muslims, Christians, Druze, Alawites, Israeli Jews, and scattered Jewish communities elsewhere all part of the mix. We need to recognise the diversity of the region's colonial experience — even if many of its national borders bear testament to the straight lines beloved of all colonial rulers. Straight borders, though, rarely make for tidy on-the-ground realities. Some states, Algeria in particular, had a long period of French rule. Others, like Saudi Arabia, were never formally colonised. Egypt has long prided itself as being a leader of both the Arab and the African worlds, which reflects both a geographic and symbolic reality. Some states (Sudan is a good example) have a decidedly mixed heritage, seen in the faces of its Arab and African peoples and, too often, in its bloody history.

If Middle Eastern diversity is reflected in the experience of the past, it is also very much a present-day reality. Take the extraordinary divergences in wealth and livelihood. The divide between the oil and the non-oil states is stark. In the oil-rich United Arab

Emirates, gross domestic product per capita at the dawn of the 21st century was around $23,000. In Yemen, a country troubled by civil war and other internal strife, it was less than $1,000. Look also at the difference in educational standards between Jordan and Djibouti. Jordan has first-world adult literacy rates both for men and women, while Djibouti struggles to achieve a female literacy rate of 55 per cent (which is still nearly twice as high as Yemen). Djibouti also scores badly on life expectancy—around 45 for men and a couple of years more for women, which is worse than the figures for many Western countries a century ago.

In the first decade of the twenty-first century, the Arab Middle East—a vast stretch of 21 countries plus the Palestinian territories of the Gaza Strip and the West Bank)—had a combined population of around 320 million people, ranging from a paltry 600,000 in Qatar to cheek-by-jowl congestion of some 75 million in Egypt. To look at a map of Egypt, the world's oldest nation state, we might think it not lacking in space. But only a tiny proportion of the Egyptian land mass is habitable.

We see the demographic weight of the Arab world most sharply in the Israeli–Palestinian contest, in which, bluntly put, Jews are being outbred by Muslims. But the issue is much broader and more complex. The Arab world is young and fertile, with high population growth rates. Take Somalia, a desperately poor country of around 10 million people, of whom nearly half are under 15, with a population growth rate of over 4 per cent and life expectancy of around 48. Elsewhere, on current projections, by 2050 Yemen will have a population larger than Russia (currently 21 million people, compared to 140 million). Leaving aside what this might mean for Russia, what will it mean for Yemen? Expand this question to other Arab states, from Algeria through Palestine to Saudi Arabia. What of food and education and jobs and housing? In the handful of oil-rich states, this may not be a huge problem. But most of the Middle East is anything but oil-wealthy. What will burgeoning populations mean for their governments' capacity to maintain control? And even in the wealthy states, population growth points to big problems ahead. Just look at the richest of them: Saudi Arabia. In the last quarter of the twentieth century its population grew by 5 per cent annually, but average per-capita income fell from nearly $29,000 to just under $7,000. Over the next 25 years the ruling House of Saud, currently totalling about 30,000 members, will double in size. How long can it go on indulging itself and buying off the population at large?

The Middle East casts a long, ominous shadow — affecting politics, economics, demographics, and security — over our world. The issues include political change and reform, encapsulated in the stuttering debate about Middle Eastern 'democratisation'. They include the question of religion—especially Islam's internal stresses—and the threats posed by Islamic extremism. We should ponder the contradiction between the US and its friends urging Arab regimes towards democracy and greater personal freedom and, at the same time, demanding that they deal firmly with terrorism. More freedom can lead to greater opportunities for wanton behaviour, directed at those very regimes. We might note, too, the paradox of Islamic extremists across the region potentially being the major beneficiaries of democratic reform that involves genuinely free elections. Outsiders, especially Americans, like to hold out a good dose of liberty as the answer to the Middle East's problems. But liberty, like medicine, needs to be administered with care. Those who subscribe to the 'hypocritic' rather than the Hippocratic oath quickly find themselves in trouble. We only have to look at contemporary Iraq to see that policies driven by ideological fixation, ignorance, and deceit are headed for disaster.

What will the Arab world and the broader Middle East region look like in 2020? We might as well start with an optimistic picture.

Scenario 1

America's successful invasion of Iraq early in the century transformed the Middle East. From modest and, at times, difficult beginnings in Iraq, democratic practice took firm hold throughout the

region. Arab liberalism is now in the ascendancy.
Religious fundamentalism has retreated, epitomised
by the popular election of a female president in
Saudi Arabia. Following the successful 'Peoples'
Revolution' in Iran, backed by the CIA, Iran
renounced its nuclear weapons program. It enjoys a
very close relationship with the US, which played a
key role in securing Iran's permanent membership
of the expanded United Nations Security Council.

The Israelis and Palestinians have been at peace
for nearly a decade. They enjoy a close economic
and security relationship under the terms of their
Treaty of Amity and Cooperation, negotiated
during the first term of US president Barak Obama.
Hundreds of thousands of Palestinians work in
Israel, and many Israelis settlers stayed in the West
Bank and the Golan Heights, respectively taking
out Palestinian and Syrian citizenship. To allay
Israeli concerns about the demographic imbalance
between their two nations, the Palestinian
government, nominally Islamic but dominated by
secularists, introduced a vigorous family planning
program. The two governments also agreed to limit
the total number of Palestinians who can be citizens
of the Jewish state. Israelis travel freely throughout
the Arab and indeed the broader Muslim world.
A superhighway is under construction, linking
Bagdad, Damascus, Beirut, Tel Aviv, Jerusalem, and

Amman, funded in part by substantial donations from the wealthy oil states. Oil revenues have benefited spectacularly from the 60 per cent increase in world consumption since the beginning of the century. Despite occasional calls outside the region for diversification of supply, the Middle East remains the world's primary source of oil, with about 70 per cent of its proven reserves.

One concern shared by all Middle Eastern states involves the supply of fresh water to meet the demands of growing populations. Under an innovative 'Oil for Water' barter program, devised by the US and Israel, massive icebergs, which are increasing in number as a result of global warming, are now towed to the Gulf. From there, the melted freshwater is piped throughout the region. Israel has also spearheaded a regional desalination program named in honour of American president George W Bush, whose vision and determination for the region made real what many saw as fantasy.

For those inclined to a less rosy view of the world, the following might seem closer to the possible reality.

Scenario 2

Following America's bloody debacle in Iraq and the palpable failure of its plans for 'moderate' democratic reform in the Middle East, a new bout

of isolationism has swept the US. Middle Eastern
politics has seen the emergence of increasingly
hardline Islamic regimes, and there are regular flare-
ups along Israel's borders with Egypt, Jordan, and
Lebanon. Frequent armed incursions from Lebanon
have forced the relocation of all civilians within a
50-kilometre strip inside Israel's northern border.
This has been declared a free-fire zone. The Golan
Heights remains nominally under Israeli control,
but is the scene of constant skirmishing between
Israeli forces and those from Syria, Lebanon, and
Iraq.

Iran is the kingmaker in the region, especially in
Iraq, where the Shia connection makes for a natural
alliance. Arab states adopt a generally deferential
approach towards Iran. This masks an intense rivalry,
driven by the Sunni/Shia divide and the fact that
Iran is not part of the Arab world.

Religious and security issues loom large. The
former centres on popular pressure within the
region for the creation of a new Sunni caliphate.
The logical home for this is Saudi Arabia; but
the Palestinians, as nominal protectors of Islamic
Jerusalem, have mounted a strong counter-claim
that the caliphate should be based there. This adds,
naturally, to Israeli alarm about the threats to its
existence posed by Islamic extremism and the
unresolved Palestinian question. Israel's anxieties

are compounded by an increasing outflow of its
citizens. This is matched by a 'brain drain' from
the Arab world as young, educated Arabs clamour
for a better life elsewhere, especially in Europe or
America.

There is increasing acrimony between Israel and
its neighbours about the sharing of dwindling water
resources. The continuing Israeli–Palestinian conflict
underpins growing debate within Israel about the
country's long-term prospects. At one level, this
involves calls for pre-emptive action against the
Arab states and the expulsion of all non-Jews living
in Israel. At another, it feeds arguments that the era
of an exclusive Jewish nation has passed, and that
Israel's only future lies in a bi-national state. Israeli
domestic politics are more fractious than ever, with
governments rarely lasting for long.

In addition to the tools of oil, religion, and
terrorism, Iran and the Arab world have gone
down the nuclear-weapons path. Iran has been the
least bashful, successfully testing several nuclear
devices, and vowing eventual retaliation for Israeli
air-raids that badly damaged several of its nuclear
production facilities. Saudi Arabia has hinted that
its Islamic bomb will help to protect the proposed
new caliphate. Egypt, Syria, and Libya are thought
to possess a nuclear-weapons capability. They have
not confirmed this, opting instead for a policy of

'constructive ambiguity', in the Israeli mode.

Oil revenues continue to be the economic lifeblood of the Arab states, funding extravagant and unproductive lifestyles for their autocratic rulers. These rulers are painted by their domestic critics as predators of the national wealth and impediments to the restoration of true Islamic values. Increasingly, they are the target of extremist violence. Compounding leadership problems is the growing incidence of AIDS and other epidemics, in the Gulf states in particular—resulting in an even greater dependence on imported foreign labour.

The Middle East in 2020 poses a greater danger to Western interests and security than at any time before. At its heart lie failed American dreams, ineffectual and internally divided European involvement, and the unsavoury internal dynamics of the Arab states themselves.

These two scenarios, admittedly, are at the extreme of probabilities. Like *The Economist's* attempt at futurology involving finance ministers, London garbagemen, and others, any prediction—optimistic or otherwise, cautious or wild—can only be a best guess. But if the past and the present are any guide to the Middle East of the future, we might hope for the first scenario, but we should prepare for the second.

CHAPTER ONE

Oil's Not Well

Anyone contemplating the world of Middle Eastern oil must pay homage to the words of former US defence secretary Donald Rumsfeld. In February 2002, he declared: 'There are things we know we know. We also know there are known unknowns ... things we do not know. But there are also unknown unknowns—the ones we don't know we don't know.' The British Plain English Campaign rightly awarded Rumsfeld a 'Foot in Mouth' prize for this stumbling insight. A campaign representative noted: 'We think we know what he means. But we don't know if we really know.'

It was easy to poke fun at Rumsfeld, a legendary language-mangler. He certainly deserved the prize, having beaten off stiff competition from heavyweights such as Arnold Schwarznenegger ('gay marriage should be between a man and a woman') and Chris Patten ('the Conservative Party had committed political suicide and was living to regret it'). Rumsfeld, nonetheless, had offered a useful framework for looking at the one product on which all human beings wittingly or unwittingly rely—oil.

There is much that we do know about oil. We know its centrality in our lives, that it is finite, that it will run out. We know its approximate distribution around the globe, and the extraordinary wealth it generates for those fortunate enough to possess it in abundance. But for all that we know, there is much that we do not. How much oil is left under our lands and seas remains a matter for sharp disagreement. So, too, is the question of how much ultimately can be exploited; when global production will peak and begin to decline; and how long it will be before we finally run out of the commodity that made the world 'modern'.

Debate over when global oil production will peak pits the 'early toppers', who argue that we are now very close, against the so-called 'late toppers', who push the date back to sometime between 2030 and 2040. Some late toppers point eagerly to the 1972 warning by the global think tank the Club of Rome that the world would run out of oil by last century's end. Since then, international oil reserves have nearly doubled, and known gas reserves have tripled. Technological advance, bringing with it the capacity to shift 'possible' reserves to 'probable' and 'probable' to 'proven' dealt the early toppers a blow, though not necessarily a mortal one.

Whether the world's oil barrel is half full or half

empty, it will, inexorably, one day, have a very hollow ring. So what on earth did *The Economist* have in mind when, under the headline 'Drowning in oil', it declared in 1999 that the world 'is awash with the stuff, and it is likely to remain so'? By that time, nearly half of the top-ten oil nations on the magazine's own list had already passed their peak year of production: Iran (1974); Venezuela (1970); Russia (1987), and Libya (1970). True, considerable comfort could be taken from the fact that the big four Middle Eastern producers—Saudi Arabia, Iraq, the United Arab Emirates (UAE), and Kuwait—were still on the right side of peak production. But the magazine's blithe suggestion that progress would be served by getting away 'from the notion that oil is scarce' was mystifyingly wrong-headed.

The Economist may simply have been having its own Rumsfeldian moment. For when it comes to oil, good sense sometimes takes a holiday. Take the bizarre phenomenon of oil experts predicting with decimal-point precision the remaining amounts of 'undiscovered' reserves. In 2003, for example, the Energy Information Agency (EIA) of the United States Department of Energy (DOE) put the Middle East's 'undiscovered' oil resources at 269.19 billion barrels. One might have thought that 'undiscovered' could have led to a little risk-taking, maybe rounding down to 269 or even up to 270. But 269.19 it was. Perhaps such precision is intended as a message to non-experts to butt out. Rather than do that, we should take an even closer interest in the role that oil plays in our lives, where it comes from, and the problematic future it poses for many of us.

The known knowns about oil are two-fold. The first is our staggering dependency on the product; the second, our staggering dependency on the Middle East as a supplier.

Without oil we would not move, we would not eat, and a good many of us would likely freeze to death. Oil delivers the bowl of rice to the pauper, and the banquet to the rich. Without it there would be no telephones, no television, and no toothpaste. There could be no such thing as globalisation, which needs movement of people and goods, as well as ideas. According to Jeremy Leggett, former oil-industry scientist turned solar energy campaigner and self-confessed 'early topper', 90 per cent of all our transportation, whether by land, air or sea, is fuelled by oil; 95 per cent of all goods in shops involve the use of oil; and 95 per cent of all our food products require oil use.

'Just to farm a single cow and deliver it to market requires six barrels of oil, enough to drive a car from New York to Los Angeles,' he says. The difference between the early and late toppers, Leggett has argued, is between sometime 'soon'—that is, before 2010—and sometime 'far away in the 2030s'. In volume, it is the 'seismic' difference between one and two trillion barrels of oil yet to exploited. Leggett set out five 'essential' though not widely recognised facts about global oil-finds: the biggest oilfields in the world were discovered more than half a century ago, either side of World War II; the peak year of oil discovery was as long ago as 1965; there were a few big discoveries in the 1970s but none since; the last year in which more oil was discovered than consumed was a quarter of a century ago; and since then there has been an overall decline.

In recent decades we have certainly become more efficient, if not necessarily wiser, in our use of oil. But the sheer weight of our demand underlines our dependency. And whatever the wishes and the warnings of advocates of diversification and 'clean' energy, our addiction to oil is worsening. At the beginning of the twentieth century, less than 5 per cent of the world's energy needs came from oil. Today, the figure is around 40 per cent. Based on (rounded) EIA estimates, world oil consumption will rise from 77 million barrels per day (bpd) in 2000 to 119 million bpd in 2025, a cumulative increase of nearly 55 per cent. Petrol consumption could double, as the number of cars increases from around 700 million to more than 1.25 billion. These figures become even starker when put alongside the record of discovery over the past three decades. Leggett noted that 80 per cent of oil produced today comes from oilfields discovered before 1973. Despite extraordinary technology and the billions of dollars spent on exploration, the industry today is finding the equivalent of 'mice', as opposed to the 'elephant fields' of yester-decade.

Oil assumed such a prominent place in our lives because it was cheap and relatively easy to exploit. This may seem a contrary statement, given the sharp economic pain inflicted on us today at the petrol pump. But compared to other sources of energy, oil is in a league of its own — the world's most efficient mobile energy-source. In his telling account of America's oil dependency, *Addicted to Oil*, Ian Rutledge commented that oil was so prized because it was in the most convenient and adaptable state, as a liquid. Its competitors, whether renewables such solar or wind power, or nuclear power, 'must be first converted into electricity, at considerable cost'. Refining crude oil into its various products was a relatively simple industrial process — 'much cheaper, for example, than converting uranium ore into electricity'.

The other known known about oil is the centrality of the Middle East as a source. The first 'oil shock' in 1973, when prices tripled, woke up the world, as *The Economist* later wrote, to the fact that its main source of energy 'had fallen into the hands of a desert sheiks, tottering democracies and unpredictable dictators'. The world would find itself 'increasingly dependent on a few unstable and unreliable Gulf countries'. By 2030, according to the International Energy Agency (IEA), Middle Eastern producers will supply 50 per cent of US oil imports, 50 per cent of Europe's, 80 per cent of China's, and 90 per cent of Japan's. The Arab states

bordering the Persian Gulf hold well over half the world's
known oil reserves: Saudi Arabia (25 per cent); Iraq (11
per cent); the UAE (9 per cent); Kuwait (9 per cent); and
Qatar (1.5 per cent). When we add Persian Iran (9 per
cent), the total nears 65 per cent. (These figures exclude
Canada's massive but problematic shale oil reserves.)

Most of the Persian Gulf states will increase their
share of world oil in the coming decades. Although
Iran's share of world production will decline to about
4 per cent by 2025, Saudi Arabia's will increase from 12
to 19 per cent; Iraq's from 3 to 4 per cent; the UAE's
from 3 to 4 per cent; and Kuwait's from 2.5 to 4 per
cent. In the early years of the twenty-first century, these
countries together produced one-quarter of the world's
oil. By 2025 their share will have increased to around 36
per cent. Their domination of world oil rests on the fact
of their vast production continuing to outstrip domestic
demand. And their importance to oil-addicted nations
takes on even greater weight when we add in Western
hunger for cheap products from countries such as China
and India, which rely increasingly on Middle Eastern
oil for their manufacture. For the US, this might add as
much as 30 to 40 per cent to the value of its direct oil
imports from the Middl East.

The known knowns of oil and the preponderance
of the Middle East lead us into less certain territory.
Although partly to do with the questions of
quantity — how much oil remains to be mapped,

tapped, and shipped—they are more to do with the region. The Institute for the Analysis of Global Security, a Washington-based think-tank, has projected that by 2020 over 80 per cent of global oil reserves will be controlled by Middle Eastern regimes. This means that:

- A handful of Middle Eastern suppliers will regain the influence they had in the 1970s, and will manipulate oil prices and world politics;
- Middle Eastern producers will continue to use their oil revenues to increase their military expenditures, fuel an arms race, and undermine regional stability;
- Corrupt, oppressive regimes will continue to use oil revenues as a means to maintain their power;
- Wealth generated by oil-rich Middle Eastern countries will continue to flow into terrorist organisations and those promoting radical Islam;
- The US will increase its military presence in the region to ensure access to the remaining oil, meaning further US entanglement in Middle East conflicts, more anti-American sentiment, and a deepening rift between the West and the Islamic world; and
- Growing Chinese intervention in the Middle East to ensure its own access to oil, and Chinese arming of Middle Eastern countries hostile to the US and its allies, will increase US–China tension.

To this unhappy picture we might add several imponderables, including the possible impact on oil supplies and therefore prices of political or other upheavals in key oil-producing countries. What if Iraq remains a nightmare; or if Islamic extremists take power in Saudi Arabia; or if a major conflict erupts between Persian Iran and the Arab world, centred on the oil-rich states bordering the Persian Gulf and threatening the vital supply-route through the narrow Straits of Hormuz? In our neo-Rumsfeldian analysis, we might also contemplate how the world might have looked if there were no oil sheikhdoms at all; if there were a more equitable spread of oil reserves around the globe; even, perhaps, if there were no such thing as oil. The world at large would obviously be a very different place. And what of the Middle East: without oil, would we pay any attention at all to the mostly barren lands that make up this vast region? It would still resonate religiously. After all, Abraham and Christ and Mohammad made their presence felt long before oil; the pyramids would still be one of the wonders of the world; the Suez canal would still be a great engineering feat. But the Middle East would rank as little more than an exotic destination for pilgrims and tourists. Oil made our world and the Middle East's centrality in it.

If oil dominates our lives, the two nations that have dominated the world of oil are America and Saudi Arabia. On the surface, it is hard to imagine two countries with less in common. One has promoted itself as the bastion of democratic freedoms, where a zealously protected right to bear arms makes Washington one the world's most murderous capitals. The other, Saudi Arabia, makes few pretensions towards liberty. It portrays itself as the soul and protector of Islam, a fiercely authoritarian theocracy with sharp restrictions on community and personal freedom. Yet oil and ideology bound the two countries together. President Roosevelt declared in February 1943 that the defence of Saudi Arabia was 'vital' to the defence of the United States. This was, in effect, a declaration that, in return for Saudi oil, the US would help keep the Soviet Union and its fellow-travellers at bay. The enemies might now be different, but the strategic imperative has changed little. Today, with about 5 per cent of the world's population, 2 per cent of the world's oil reserves, and a thirst for one-quarter of world oil production, America's oil-driven focus on Middle Eastern suppliers is sharper than ever.

The US's oil craving is gargantuan. So, too, is its domestic production, which remains in the world's top three. In 1950, America consumed about one million barrels per day (bpd) more than it produced. The oil price shocks of the 1970s and early 1980s helped to contain demand, and to improve the balance between imports and domestic production. From the second half of the 1980s, however, increasing domestic demand and decreasing domestic production set the US on the course of the previously unthinkable. In 1998, for the first time ever, America found itself reliant on imports for more than half of its oil needs. By the end of the twentieth century the shortfall was 11 million bpd. By 2020, according to the US Department of Energy, the gap will reach 18 million bpd, or almost 70 per cent of domestic needs. Just as disturbing for Americans as the deficit is their increasing reliance on Middle Eastern oil. Currently, the Middle East provides about 20 per cent of total US consumption—a figure set to increase dramatically in the years ahead.

In 1992, president George Bush senior, a reluctant participant at the Rio 'Earth Summit', declared that the 'American Way of Life' was 'not negotiable'. America's love of the car could only have been uppermost in his mind. America is the most highly motorised country in the world, with vehicle ownership more than 50 per cent higher than in Western Europe. Since the 1950s ushered in mass car ownership, the percentage of oil consumption by the US transportation sector has risen by around 15 per cent. This figure includes motor vehicles, railways, shipping, and aircraft; given increases in wealth and population, it may not seem all that remarkable. What is startling is that, at the turn of the twenty-first century, motor vehicles alone accounted for over 50 per cent of America's total oil consumption. In *Addicted to Oil*, Rutledge commented that, for the past 40 years, the automobile 'has imprinted itself upon the psychology and personality of the American citizen to a degree which no other society has experienced'. Americans drove to and from school, work, worship, shopping malls and friends and relatives' homes. They 'refuelled not only their cars at drive-in service stations, but also their bodies at drive-through restaurants. They even had access to drive-through dry-cleaning, pharmacies, and funeral-home visitations.'

Like the elder George Bush, America's motorists just did not want to get it. Rutledge noted a despairing comment by the *Financial Times* correspondent in Washington, a few day's after Iraq's 1990 invasion of Kuwait, that the American domestic response to the Gulf crisis had 'shown a combination of childishness and evasion of reality so complete that serious political leadership no longer seems possible in this poll-dominated democracy'. American motorists already enjoyed by far the cheapest fuel in the developed world; yet, to listen to the phone-ins, an increase of 10 cents would be 'an intolerable threat to life, liberty, and the pursuit of happiness'. Americans seemed much more willing to risk blood and treasure in foreign military adventures than to 'face the bill for self-reliance'. Depressingly noteworthy here is the fact that, in the 10 years after the first Gulf War, US oil consumption increased by an all-time record, to reach just under 20 million barrels per day in the year 2000.

True, America's oil dependency was the subject of

high-sounding undertakings. Take these noble words from president Jimmy Carter:

> I am tonight setting a clear goal for the energy policy of the United States. Beginning this moment, this nation will never use more foreign oil than we did in 1977—never. From now on, every new addition to our demand for energy will be met from our own production and our own conservation. The generation-long growth in our dependence on foreign oil will be stopped dead in its tracks right now and then reversed as we move through the 1980s, for I am tonight setting the further goal of cutting our dependence on foreign oil by one-half by the end of the next decade.

Carter's declaration of independence from foreign oil was made on 15 July 1979. The following year, *the gap between domestic production and consumption grew to six million barrels a day, around double the figure it had been ten years earlier.* Today, the lip-service remains as predictable as rising foreign oil imports. In his state of the union address in early 2006, president George W Bush offered the less-than-startling insight that America was 'addicted to oil … often imported from unstable parts of the world'. This reflected the reality, which Michael Klare noted in Blood and Oil, that US reliance on foreign petroleum, much of it from the Gulf and other conflict-prone areas, 'exposes us to a host of perils, including supply disruptions, unsavoury alliances, and entanglements in deadly oil wars ... The farther we head into the future, the deeper our reliance on imported energy will be and the greater the perils we will face'.

But new technologies, president Bush declared, offered the best way of breaking this dangerous addiction. They would help America reach the 'great goal' of replacing 'more than 75 per cent of our oil imports from the Middle East by 2025 ... [of making] our dependence on Middle Eastern oil a thing of the past'. If the president was serious, one of the first things he should have done was to abolish the US Department of Energy (DOE). At the very least, he might have demanded that the department cease its unwelcome projections. According to the DOE, oil imports as a percentage of total US consumption will rise from 55 per cent in 2001 to 58 per cent in 2010, and to a staggering 75 per cent by 2025. To add insult to injury, the DOE forecasts a doubling of imports from the Gulf region, from just under three million barrels per day in 2002 to almost six million bpd by 2025. Common to both the White House and the DOE projections are the figures 75 and 2025. But the difference in their meaning could hardly be sharper.

Few people probably took president Bush's comments seriously. They were a call for diversification, not preservation; a statement of foreign or security policy, not energy policy. The president was deathly silent on fuel taxes — the tax take in the US being a mere 23 per cent of petrol prices, compared to nearly 70 per cent in the UK. Rather than wean Americans off cars, he was proposing to wean cars off the Middle East. The addict would not kick the habit; rather, he would just change dealers. There is a simple, straightforward way for Americans to reduce their dependency on oil and the Middle East: drive shorter distances in more fuel-efficient vehicles. The prospect that this might happen in any substantive way should not be a cause for sleepless nights in the oil sheikdoms.

With the vigour of those who have seen the light, Jeremy Leggett has argued that the US government could wipe out the need for all its Middle Eastern oil imports, and 'staunch the flow of much blood in the process,' by requiring domestic industry to increase the fuel efficiency of cars and light trucks. Instead, 'it allows General Motors and the rest to build ever more oil-profligate vehicles'.

America's addiction sounds like good news for Gulf producers, the Saudis in particular. Still, the president's remarks gave them momentary pause for thought, especially given the post 9/11 strains in US–Saudi relations, US suspicions about the kingdom's commitment to fighting rather than spreading Muslim extremism, and Saudi resentment at the US tendency to declare first and discuss later. The then Saudi ambassador to the US, Prince Turki al-Faisal, told CNN he was taken aback. Saudi oil minister Ali al-Naimi, was concerned at 'all the talk about not wanting our oil'. This could deter investors in Saudi Arabia's planned expansion of production capacity to 12.5 million bpd by 2009, in part to meet increasing American demand. (DOE projections show Saudi Arabia having to double its production by 2020 to meet US and world demand.)

Commenting on the Bush statement, the International Energy Agency head, Claude Mandil, spoke of his organisation's delight that the president had at last recognised 'that his country is addicted to oil'. Mandil implied, nonetheless, that such an admission was a double-edged sword. Even if the US reduced its own dependency on Middle Eastern oil, others would not. In order to supply these needs, greater investment was badly needed. The IEA estimates that, by 2030, Persian Gulf producers will have to spend more than $500 billion on new equipment and technology to meet growing demand. President Bush's remarks, Mandil said, would 'not help us convince those countries' to find these vast sums.

Assume for a moment that the US succeeded in reducing its dependency on Middle Eastern, especially Saudi, oil. Would this make any difference to the kingdom? The answer is probably very little economically, though potentially it might be significant in political and strategic terms. Even if America freed itself from the need for Saudi oil, that oil would find a ready market elsewhere, especially in developing Asia. In particular, India and China's combined consumption will increase by more than 150 per cent over the next 25 years. China, a net oil exporter until 1993, is following a much-speeded-up version of the American experience. The growth in Chinese demand for oil has been extraordinary—increasing by more than one million bpd each year (some 40 per cent of the total increase in global demand). In 2000, oil provided about 30 per cent of China's energy needs, and is likely to have risen to 50 per cent by 2010. By 2030, China's oil imports will match those of the United States. China, too, is developing an addiction to the motor car, the numbers of which are increasing by about 20 per cent each year. And while China has tried to diversify its oil-supply sources, it too is hooked on Arab oil. The IEA has estimated that China's dependency on Middle Eastern oil will rise to around 70 per cent of its total oil imports over the next decade. Saudi Arabia will prove almost as important an oil well to China as it is to the US.

This puts major Middle Eastern oil producers, especially the Saudis, in a curious position. They are the bride whose affections are sought by several suitors, each with something attractive to offer. The Americans can offer protection. It comes at a price, however: occasional hectoring about the need for 'reform' of Saudi politics. But proclaiming democratic virtues too vigorously involves risks for the US. Taken to its logical extreme, it might mean the end of the Saudi ruling family. This would certainly not be in the family's interests, let alone America's. So a 'little bit of pregnancy' is in order. As long as the US relies on Middle Eastern suppliers for a growing proportion of its oil imports, in which Saudi Arabia has the lion's share, it has a keen interest in the security of the Saudi state and in the wellbeing of Saudi's rulers. Their nepotism, corruption, and anti-democratic behaviour are a secondary consideration.

For the US, and other oil addicts, the harsh truth is that, whatever the future of Iraqi oil, Saudi Arabia will remain too important to ignore. Today, about half of total oil exports from the Arabian Gulf originate in Saudi Arabia. With or without a single drop of Saudi oil flowing into America, Saudi Arabia can influence the price of petrol at American bowsers like no other foreign government can. It is the world's only 'swing producer', with a capacity to reduce or increase production and, therefore, to shift prices one way or the other. The country plans to lift its production capacity to 13 million bpd by 2012. This is aimed at creating around 3.5 million bpd of 'spare' production to counter Iran's threat to respond to any UN sanctions by refusing to export oil, thereby further driving up prices. As well as Iran, the extra oil could also make up for Iraq, Nigeria, and Venezuela. In the careful words of Nawaf Obaid, head of the Saudi National Security Assessment Project, all four countries are 'susceptible to supply disruptions'.

Saudi Arabia wants to ensure that, 'even in the worst case scenario, global oil demand can be met'.

Happily for Americans, much of the money they put into Saudi coffers flows back. The proceeds from Saudi oil have been a bonanza for American business, especially arms manufacturers and those providing construction, communication, and oil-industry equipment. In the last half of the twentieth century, two-way trade between Saudi Arabia and the United States grew by around 70 per cent a year to reach almost $20 billion in 2000. Data compiled by the Congressional Research Service shows that international arms deliveries to Saudi Arabia between 1998 and 2005 totalled $50 billion, of which one-third came from the United States. There is also another consideration for the Americans. As long as Saudi remains oil rich—which it will do for the rest of this century—it has a substantial capacity to shape regional events, meaning relations or non-relations with Israel; the containment of Iran; events on the ground in Iraq; and attitudes towards the United States in the Arab and broader Sunni Muslim world (especially Indonesia, Malaysia, India, and Pakistan).

The events of 9/11 produced a strong anti-Saudi reaction in the US. A briefing to a Pentagon advisory board, for example, described the kingdom as 'the kernel of evil'. It recommended that the Saudis be warned to stop backing terrorism, or else face the seizure of their oilfields. The conservative commentator William Kristol excoriated the Saudi leadership for being 'part of the problem, not part of the solution'. He argued that, in pursuing its interests in the Persian Gulf, America had 'always hoped for a regional partner: first Iran, then Iraq, then the Saudis'. Each had 'proven itself incapable of the job' (note no suggestion here of any American failings).

Post 9/11, the eyes of the US administration became increasingly focused on Iraq. It seemed to offer several happy possibilities: punishing Saddam for his various crimes of commission and omission; reminding the Saudi leadership of US willingness to use its military muscle against those who threatened or offended it; and taking out oil-supply 'insurance' against a future Islamist takeover in Saudi Arabia. The last point had the added attraction that, of any major producer, Iraq has the longest period to run before peak oil production. It holds about 11 per cent of the world's known reserves, against Saudi Arabia's massive 25 per cent. But, on current projections, Saudi production peaked in 2008. This will not happen in Iraq until 2017.

What better way, Rutledge asked in Addicted to Oil, to 'hedge' against the possibility that Saudi Arabia might sooner or later fall to the Islamists or others hostile to the US than to take control of an adjacent Gulf country, so richly endowed with oil resources? And if such a strategy 'simultaneously opened hugely profitable oilfields to American capital, gave intense satisfaction to the Israelis, could legitimately be portrayed worldwide as the removal of cruel tyrant, and at the same time taught the militant Islamists a serious lesson about the true reach of American power, then so much the better'. In the short-lived triumphalism after Saddam Hussein's overthrow, an America oil industry consultant declared: 'We have a new ally in the Middle East—one that is secular, modern and pro free market ... It's time to replace the Saudis with the Iraqis'. Such is the stuff of oil dreams.

Leave aside the disastrous consequences for many Iraqis of the invasion of their homeland, and the gift that America and its allies handed to Iran through the empowerment of Iraq's Shia majority. One question we should ask is whether the American-led occupation has enhanced the prospects of an Islamist revolution in Saudi Arabia. Even by official American admission, Iraq became a magnet for Islamist fanatics, providing an ideal environment for their recruitment and on-the-job training. Once America and its allies withdraw from Iraq, whatever spin-doctored language is used to disguise the retreat, will these fanatics turn their gaze determinedly towards Saudi Arabia? Will the occupation of Iraq prove to be a defeat on two fronts: a failure to secure Iraq as counter to Saudi's Arabia's oil power, and a means of furthering the prospects of an Islamist takeover in Saudi itself?

Robert Baer, ex-CIA and long-time Saudi watcher and critic, has written that the US approach to Saudi

Arabia was built on the delusion that the kingdom was stable, and that both the regime and the flow of oil could continue indefinitely. Not all the wishing in the world, Baer wrote, would change the basic reality that:

- Saudi Arabia controls the largest share of the world's oil, and serves as the market regulator for the global petroleum industry;
- No country consumes more oil, and is more dependent on Saudi oil, than the United States;
- The US and the rest of the industrialised world are therefore absolutely dependent on Saudi Arabia's oil reserves, and will be for decades to come;
- If the Saudi oil spigot is shut off, by terrorism or by political revolution, the effect on the global and particularly the US economy will be devastating; and
- Saudi oil is controlled by an increasingly bankrupt, criminal, dysfunctional, and out-of-touch royal family that is hated by the people it rules and by the nations that surround its kingdom.

Whatever the criticisms, the Saudi regime knows that it remains in the driver's seat. It has vast quantities of cheaply exploitable oil. Whatever the vagaries of American needs, other buyers are eager to soak up its production. And America's oil addiction will help to ensure wariness on the part of US administrations in pushing the Saudis too far. In late 2006, Prince Turki al-Faisal warned against American 'rhetoric and bombast' when it came to criticising Saudi Arabian society and politics. While reform was on the agenda, 'we're not going to change just because you tell us to do so ... we will do so in our own way, in accordance with our traditions and culture'. What really matters to American administrations is their own political health, not the niceties or otherwise of Saudi politics. They will not jeopardise the former for the sake of the latter. Moreover, even if the US weaned itself entirely off Saudi and Middle Eastern oil—a fanciful prospect—Middle Eastern producers would remain the critical players in determining international oil supplies and prices. The harsh reality is that major non-Middle Eastern producers are rapidly approaching burnout. If production continues at today's rates—which is more than likely—large producers in the recent past such as Russia, America, Norway, and China will be bit players within a couple of decades.

Worse still, for those who would like to see the world less dependent on Middle Eastern oil, is the fact that it is not just about production, but also about refinery capacity. Middle Eastern oil states aim to increase their profits through increasing their exports of refined oil products, helped here by the increasing resistance of major oil importers to the building of new refineries because of environmental concerns. In 1990, Middle

Eastern refinery capacity was five million bpd, around 8 per cent of world capacity. The IEA projects a doubling to 10 million bpd by 2010 and to nearly 16 million bpd by 2030, or 13 per cent of the world total. Saudi Arabia has ambitious plans to double its refinery capacity through joint ventures in China, South Korea, and on its own soil to reach six million bpd in the next few years. Antony Cordesman, a forensic analyst of Middle Eastern affairs, has noted that such a shift in refinery capacity can lead 'to greater dependence on a given Middle Eastern supplier because it produces precisely the product for a given commercial need'. It can also reduce the capacity to substitute Middle Eastern oil, as 'there may be no source of similar refinery or production capacity'.

Middle Eastern countries are also well placed to provide an energy-hungry world with natural gas, global demand for which is likely to almost double within the next two decades. Known reserves of gas in the broader Middle East have more than doubled in the past two decades. The region now holds 40 per cent of the world's total, the major sources being Iran (second only to Russia in volume), Qatar, Saudi Arabia, and the UAE. These reserves play a critical role in cushioning domestic oil consumption, thereby leaving more oil for export. Domestic oil consumption is projected to increase by about 2 per cent annually until 2025. Without the availability of gas, the figure would be three times this level.

America's need for Middle Eastern oil, now and into the future, gives it an intense focus on the region. This reflects not merely its immediate national concerns, but its interests, selfish or otherwise, in the political, strategic, and economic wellbeing of its friends in Europe and Japan, who share its thirst for imported oil. The uncomfortable reality for America and its allies is that, every day, millions of barrels of the commodity that keeps the world working pass in giant tankers through the Straits of Hormuz, the narrow, troubled waters between Saudi Arabia and Iran. Since World War II, US presidents have been anything but averse to ordering military action in the Middle East. This may have been dressed up in the rhetoric of creating a better, safer world, but the strategic reality was all too evident. President Jimmy Carter had high hopes of ending America's oil-import dependency. But he also recognised, in 1980, that access to the Persian Gulf was a national interest to be protected 'by any means necessary, including military force'. This decades- old reality will not change anytime soon. Noting the Pentagon's creation of a central command to control all US military operations in the Persian Gulf arena, Michael Klare wrote that its principal task was to protect the global flow of petroleum. Slowly but surely, he argued, 'the US military is being converted into a global oil-protection service'.

Whatever the hopes of advocates of alternate energy, and the pronouncements of governments driven by a mix of idealism and cynical politics, the world and its people have too much at stake in the wherewithal of the oil age — from cars, to computers, to condoms. Whatever the precise mix of reasons for America's invasion of Iraq, it held out the prospect of reducing its exposure to the frailties of Saudi politics and that country's oil clout. The harsh truth, though, is that American oil ambitions for Iraq are unattainable as long as chaos persists. Rather than lessening its dependency on Saudi Arabia and increasing its energy security, the Americans have achieved the opposite. Occupation of Arab land by America and its allies, and the fillip this gave Islamist extremists, has increased the risk of turmoil in Iraq and beyond, including Saudi Arabia.

Oil has provided unimaginable wealth for a small group of Middle Eastern rulers: none of them democratic, few of them seemingly at ease with Western notions of equality for all, and personal freedom. Paradoxically, these same rulers are guardians of one of the great monotheistic religions — Islam — which preaches equality before God. The opulent lifestyle of the privileged few directly contradicts the behaviours they are expected to uphold. Here, oil plays a critical role. For if it offers opportunities for extravagance, it also provides the means to buy quiet — a 'social contract' between rulers who can enjoy the good life, providing they allow enough oil revenue to trickle down to buy the quiescence of the population at large. As usual, Saudi

Arabia provides some of the best examples of the worst behaviour. The extended Al-Saud ruling family is now estimated to total around 30,000 people, of whom about one-quarter are princes. As only a very small minority have any real role in government, the obvious question is, what do the rest do? The obvious answer is, they work hard spending their pocket money. According to *The Economist*, 'even lowly princes are believed to receive a monthly stipend of at least $10,000'.

In *Addicted to Oil*, Ian Rutledge noted that the die for self-indulgent living was cast early in Saudi's rise to oil prominence. The royal family treated national oil revenues essentially as personal income. It bought a yacht for $3 million; later, in an apparent acknowledgement that no-one was interested in sailing, the yacht was sold at a bargain-basement price. Lavish palaces were built, the catering bill for which ran into tens of millions of dollars. An IMF study of the Saudi economy in 2000 estimated oil-export receipts at $72 billion, yet 'the published Saudi budget only acknowledged receipts of $57 billion'. There were no prizes for guessing where the missing billions went. Saudi arms' purchases also offered grand opportunities for those close to power. In 2005, Saudi military spending, at $25 billion, was the eighth-highest in the world, well ahead of Israel at $9.6 billion and Iran at a relatively modest $7 billion. Saudi Arabia has legitimate security concerns, whether about Iran, Iraq—both during Saddam Hussein's rule and after his downfall—and the need to maintain domestic order against the threat from extremist Islam. But a purple haze of corruption hangs about its arms-purchasing process. Rutledge wrote that arms contracts provided one of the largest and most easily concealed sources of income for another 'army' made up of 'the ever-multiplying host of corrupt princelings and their hangers-on whose sumptuous living conditions were funded from the huge pay-offs made by Western companies'.

A window opened on this with media reports that Britain's Serious Fraud Office (SFO) was investigating an alleged slush fund of nearly $120 million set up by Britain's biggest defence contractor, BAE Systems, to provide members of the Saudi royal family with luxury holidays and cars, including a gold Rolls-Royce and other necessities of the high life. Saudi authorities 'hit the roof' on learning that a Swiss magistrate had been persuaded to force disclosure of details of confidential Swiss bank accounts. BAE's stake in smooth business relations with Saudi Arabia was underlined by the approximately $80 billion worth of business it and its partners had done with the kingdom over the previous two decades.

In late 2006, the British attorney-general, Lord Goldsmith, announced that the SFO was 'discontinuing' the investigation. This move, according to the SFO, followed 'representations that have been made both to the Attorney General and the Director of the

SFO concerning the need to safeguard national and international security'. The relief felt by the British and Saudi governments and BAE must have soured considerably in April 2008 when the High Court delivered a stinging rebuke to the SFO, following pressure for a judicial review from two advocacy groups. The court ruled that, in dropping the investigation, the British government and the SFO had 'failed to recognise the rule of law'. Discontinuing the investigation may have avoided 'uncomfortable consequences, both commercial and diplomatic', but it also aroused 'fear for the reputation of the administration of justice if it can be perverted by a threat'. In a clear reference to Saudi pressure to drop the case, one judge observed that no one, 'whether within this country or outside, is entitled to interfere in the course of justice'.

Given that Islam prohibits wasteful consumption or profligacy, it is easy for internal and external Islamist critics to excoriate Saudi Arabia's rulers for their oil-driven, un-Islamic ways. From the fat stipends paid to an ever-increasing royal family, the often-obscene extravagance of the ruling family's lifestyle, and the charade that passes for the Saudi national budget, Islamist and other critics are presented daily with more cause for complaint. So is Saudi Arabia ripening or indeed now ripe for Islamist revolution, fed by the sins of commission and omission of those in power? This question leads us, inexorably, to another: what if? What impact would an Islamist takeover of Saudi Arabia have on its oil industry? In 1998, Osama bin Laden declared that the 'correct' price of oil should be $144 a barrel. This was about twelve times the then going rate, though eerily prophetic by today's prices. How bin Laden thought this increase should to be achieved, and his intentions for the extra revenues, were not made clear.

Given Saudi Arabia's centrality in the oil industry, the reverberations of an Islamist takeover of the country would be felt world-wide. The natural inclination of an Islamist regime might be to punish America and its friends through a ban on oil sales. Given the growth in oil demand in Asia, though, this would not necessarily lead to a significant drop in Saudi oil revenues. But an Islamist regime would have other factors to consider. It would almost certainly find itself at loggerheads with Iran, just as much as Saudi's current rulers. So, from both a Saudi and American perspective, the strategic reality underlying the relationship — America's need for oil, and Saudi Arabia's need for protection — would not automatically change with the fall of the house of Saud. The imponderables would not just be on the Saudi side. One obvious question is the extent to which the US would want to continue to do business with an Islamist-run Saudi Arabia. Would its distaste be such that, finally, and paradoxically, it would find the stomach for a serious focus on non-oil energy for American cars and industry?

An Islamist-run Saudi Arabia would face three options: continue current oil-production levels; increase them; or reduce them. The choice would not necessarily be straightforward. The first is perhaps the most obvious. After all, an Islamist regime would want to generate sufficient funds to secure its hold on power. This might offer comfort to Western and other oil importers who wish neither for disruption in supplies nor rising and unstable prices. But this choice could pose a threat to Western interests, for it would generate income that might be used to support terror or other networks opposed to these interests. Such a threat would increase if oil exports increased—provided this was done in a way that avoided flooding the market and depressing prices.

Reducing oil production might offer Islamists an all-round win. Arguably, a strict application of Islamic principles warrants a slower rate of extraction than has been applied by Saudi Arabia (and some other Muslim nations), where oil revenues have funded lives of unimaginable opulence for a few. Yet turning the tap down would not necessarily have a dramatic impact on total oil revenues. Less oil on the world market could well push up prices. So an Islamist regime could choose to reduce supplies and still generate ample revenues to pursue its domestic and foreign goals. In effect, the regime could have its oil in the ground, its money in the bank, and its theological purity intact.

Oil pervades our daily life. It draws us to the often-unappealing realities of the Middle East. Even without an Islamist takeover in Saudi Arabia, the world of Middle Eastern oil is likely to become increasingly complicated and insecure for Western players. We might recall here *The Economist*'s comment, quoted earlier, about the impact of the first oil price shock of 1973 in waking up the world to the centrality of the Middle East. Little has changed in the 35 years since, except that industrialised, oil-importing nations are now competing with emerging major economies such as India and China for the favours of countries that remain corrupt and authoritarian. An uncomfortable truth for the West is that booming Asian demand for Middle Eastern oil is likely to reduce that region's own 'dependence' on the US and its friends as oil export-markets. In turn, this may well lessen Western influence and commercial reach into the Middle East. China's insatiable demand for Middle Eastern oil will also dampen Arab sensibilities about the state of the relationship with the US, further weakening the impact of the US's ill-delivered democratisation campaign. Iran, ironically, might help the US by adding to the jitteriness of autocratic Sunni Muslim regimes and keeping them in the American fold.

In May 1957, Rear Admiral Hyman Rickover delivered a prescient speech at a banquet of the Minnesota State Medical Association. Warning of the dangers to America and to the world of the dependency on non-renewable fossil fuels, he observed that 'our energy base differs from that of all earlier civilisations. They could have maintained their energy supply by careful cultivation. We cannot.' Burned fossil fuel was gone forever. The difference between pessimistic and optimistic forecasts of fossil-fuel reserves was a matter of generations or, at best, a century or two—a relatively short time in history. Fifty years on from Rickover's speech, and drawing on our Rumsfeldian analytical tool, we should put aside the unknowns. For the known knowns of oil supply over the next quarter century already give us enough cause for concern. They may not impinge on individual or collective consciousness in the same way that terrorism or weapons of mass destruction do. But they will give us equally sleepless nights.

CHAPTER TWO

Neither Free, nor Civil

DEATH NOTICE

Friends and supporters of Arab democracy are invited
to mourn its passing. Few can claim to have known it
well, though some spoke about it warmly. Its life upon
this cynical earth was all too brief.

For some outsiders, the Middle East for much of the
twentieth century must have seemed a world apart:
a world of men clad in flowing gowns and curious
headwear; of women draped in no-nonsense black; of
dramatic, harsh landscapes in which the misshapen beast
known as the camel was a logical fit; and of sheikhs
and imams and other exotic-sounding terms, and the
muezzin's haunting call to prayer.

True, placenames such as Bethlehem and Nazareth
and Jerusalem held resonances for many beyond the
region—resonances that helped to anchor their lives.

True, also, that much of the outside world ran on the oil supplied by the countries of this mysterious region, and that this dependency sometimes delivered sharp stabs of financial pain. True, too, that the often-compelling conflict between Jew and Arab over Israel's rebirth could not be ignored. But to be broadly aware of these matters hardly amounted to scrutiny about how the Arab Middle East was governed. Neither did it reflect concern about the welfare of its peoples, nor comprehension of the region's tensions and pressure points, and possible future directions. As long as the oil flowed, and the violence, though occasionally horrific, was confined mainly to Arab and Jew — or Arab and Iranian, in the case of the brutal war in which the West backed Saddam Hussein against Ayatollah Khomeini's newly founded theocratic state — the Middle East could be tucked into the recesses of the mind.

Then, on 11 September 2001, the Arab Middle East found itself propelled onto world centre stage. The awful events of that morning included the struggle of passengers and crew against the hijackers of United Flight 93, which was doomed to crash into a field in Pennsylvania. This would be cast by some Americans, president George W Bush included, as the first counterattack of World War III.* By deduction,

---

* Curiously, Norman Podhoretz, long-time editor of the conservative *Commentary* magazine and self-described

Arabs—especially the 15 Saudi Arabian nationals among the 9/11 hijackers—had started the third global conflict. This conflict, in president Bush's ill-chosen words, would involve a new crusade to remake the Arab and Islamic worlds.

America's first target was the non-Arab, medievally minded Taliban regime in Afghanistan. Most in the West—and many in Afghanistan itself—applauded its overthrow. Even the glaring failure to rid the world of Osama bin Laden's whispery, menacing presence became an unremarkable footnote. America hung the Afghanistan scalp on its belt and moved on to Iraq. There lay the seeds of what would become a grand experiment to transform the Middle East. Initially, though, toppling Saddam was not about saving the Arab world but ridding the wider one of the threat of his arsenal of weapons of mass destruction (WMD). Embarrassingly, none could be found. So another rationale was needed to explain American actions. What more noble cause could there be than that of democratising Arabs—of using Iraq as the first 'domino', a launching pad to free 300 million-plus people from the burden of their corrupt and dictatorial rulers? And, unlike the discredited

---

founder-father of neoconservatism, has argued that World War III ended victoriously in 1990 with the collapse of the Soviet Union. According to Podhoretz, we are now fighting World War IV. It would seem hard to win a war if you don't know which one it is.

domino theory of the 1960s, which foresaw an unerring communist advance throughout South-East Asia, and which led to almost 60,000 American military deaths, the new domino theory would be a force for good. A tsunami of liberal reform would sweep away the rulers of the Arab world, securing the interests of America and its 'free world' allies. The Arab world, birthplace of the three great monotheistic religions, home of modern science and astronomy and mathematics, had sunk into a deep and dangerous torpor. America would be its Prince Charming, delivering the kiss of freedom.

If any region lay ripe for this kiss it was certainly the Arab Middle East. In the last quarter of the twentieth century the number of democracies around the globe had almost tripled. Democratic practice had grown everywhere—but not in the Middle East. There, authoritarianism remained rampant, offering great opportunity for those on top of the pile. A glance at who owned what highlighted the breath-taking wealth of Middle Eastern autocrats, for whom Western notions of transparency and accountability were the stuff of nightmares. A list of the world's ten richest heads of state published by *Forbes* magazine in 1999 placed the Sultan of Brunei first, Queen Beatrix of the Netherlands seventh, and England's Queen Elizabeth tenth. All the remainder were Arab autocrats: King Fahd, Saudi Arabia, $28 billion; Sheikh Zayed Ibn Sultan, Abu Dhabi, $20 billion; Prince Jaber, Kuwait, $17 billion; Sheikh

Makhtoum, Dubai, $12 billion; Saddam Hussein, Iraq, $6 billion; Prince Hamad, Qatar, $5 billion; president Hafiz al-Assad, Syria, $2 billion. How had these fabulous fortunes been accumulated — by sweat of brow and thrift alone? How effectively had they been used to improve the lot of millions of fellow countrymen and women? How, with such wealth so readily to hand, was the Middle East, collectively, seen to be so backward? In the last quarter of the twentieth century, average per-capita income in the Arab world had grown by a mere half a per cent annually — less than half the global average.

None of this had unduly worried American administrations. But after 9/11, and especially with Saddam gone and his lack of WMD embarrassingly on display, democratisation and accountability became the cutting edge of America's approach to the Arab world. In 2003, president Bush's 'forward strategy of freedom' asked rhetorically whether the peoples of the Middle East were 'somehow beyond the reach of liberty?' The answer, of course, was no, because, according to a later Bush explanation, God had 'planted in every human the desire to live in [presumably American-style] freedom'. The Almighty had also put George W in the White House to lead democracy's charge.

As America turned its attention and considerable energies towards the task of democratising the Middle East, the picture before it was decidedly mixed. A taskforce created by the influential Council on Foreign Relations (CFR) and co-chaired by former US secretary of state Madelaine Albright reported that the Middle East was often seen as 'democracy's desert'. Internal pressures for change and the emergence of a new generation of young, dynamic leaders such as Jordan's King Abdallah II, Bahrain's King Hamad bin Isa al-Khalifa, the Qatari Emir Sheikh Hamad bin Khalifa al-Thani, and Morocco's King Mohamed VI, had produced some liberalisation. The taskforce's shopping list of democratic good news included Bahrain convening its parliament for the first time since 1975; Algerians re-electing president Abdelaziz Bouteflika in balloting that met the European Union's standards, despite 'some irregularities'; Qatar promulgating a constitution giving its citizens new political rights and establishing a 45-seat Consultative Assembly, two-thirds of which was open to direct election; Saudi Arabia taking the 'very limited step' of holding its first nationwide municipal elections; Kuwait's parliament approving the right of women to vote 'after years of refusing to do so'; and the Egyptian president, Hosni Mubarak, agreeing to amend the country's constitution to allow contested presidential elections.

The taskforce wisely acknowledged the 'superficial quality' of many of these changes. They had not fundamentally altered the prevailing, non-democratic rules of the political game. The list of minuses was just as long as the plusses. The 2004 Qatar constitution, for example, institutionalised the power of the emir and the ruling Al Thani family. Three Saudis who had circulated a petition advocating a constitutional monarchy—as opposed to the existing absolute one—were sentenced to between six and nine years in prison. Bahraini authorities made much of the return of the country's legislature after a 27-year absence, but still arrested human-rights activists and bloggers critical of the government. Amendments to the Egyptian constitution hardly risked an effective challenge to President Mubarak, and he wasted little time in proving this correct. In September 2005, Mubarak was re-elected for a fifth six-year term, against nine other candidates. His share of the vote, at just under 89 per cent, represented a mere 5 per cent decline from the 1999 'election', when he was the only nominee. Perhaps emboldened by this, and fearful of the Muslim Brotherhood's growing electoral appeal, Mubarak demonstrated his commitment to democracy by postponing municipal elections.

The Council on Foreign Relations drew attention to the continuing problems of governance in the Arab world: the 'overwhelming power of unelected heads of state'; bureaucratic inertia; the lack of rule of law; the absence of a free press; weak political parties; and, 'of course, the outsized role of security services in politics and society'. The justification for this miserable state of affairs had 'long been national security, notably the perceived Israeli threat and the problem of Islamist extremism'. Valid security concerns were 'consistently used to thwart legitimate opposition'. The continuing suppression of activists and the unveiling of 'reform' policies 'with little substance showed the determination of Arab leaders to manage political pressure rather than to risk changes 'that would alter the authoritarian nature of their political systems'.

As some Americans were detailing the Arab world's democratic shortcomings so, too, were important voices within the region itself. Few better examples could be found than the Arab Human Development (AHD) reports. Prepared under the auspices of the United Nations Development Program, these reports provided a refreshingly candid account of Arab problems. The first report, in 2002, painted a stark picture of backwardness: 10 million school-age children were not in classrooms, and some 65 million Arab adults could not read or write. This report, and later ones, gave a sharp reminder of the huge economic and human disparities across the Arab world. The third report, issued in 2004, noted that per-capita incomes ranged from $870 in Yemen to almost $22,500 in the United Arab Emirates (UAE); adult literacy rates varied from an admirable 91 per cent in Jordan to a mere 41 per cent in Mauritania; life expectancy for men ranged from 45 years in Djibouti to 75 in Kuwait and, for women, from 47 in Djibouti to 79 in Kuwait. Responding to the AHD report's stark critique of political, economic, and social realities, the US secretary of state, Condoleeza Rice, asked how such a great a region of the world, the cradle of civilisation which 'led human progress for so many years', could barely produce a combined gross domestic product equal to that of Spain. The explanation, unsurprisingly, lay in 'the absence of freedom and the absence of liberty'.

Reflecting on his influential 'end of history' thesis, Francis Fukuyama, too, drew a strong link between economic development and the growth of democratic institutions. When a country passed a per-capita income level of about $6,000 it was no longer an agricultural society, and was likely to have a property-owning middle class, a complex civil society, and mass education. All these factors, said Fukuyama, tended 'to promote the desire for democratic participation, and thus drive, from the bottom up, the demand for democratic political institutions'. Applied to the Arab world, such an economic determinist argument fell over before it got to the starting line. In 2002, for example, those countries with per-capita incomes in excess of $6,000 were Tunisia, Libya, Saudi Arabia, Oman, Kuwait, Bahrain, Qatar, and the UAE. The prospects for meaningful democratic reform in any of them were remote. Conversely, the two countries often held up as most promising for such change—Jordan and Morocco—had per-capita incomes respectively of about $4,000. In Jordan, King Abdullah had commissioned a group of prominent locals to draw up a reform agenda. They produced a 2,500-page program. All it really led to, unfortunately, was a photo opportunity.

Politics across the Arab world has long been delivered in different packaging, from the presidential republics of Algeria, Egypt, Sudan, Syria, and Tunisia to the traditional monarchies of Bahrain, Jordan, Morocco, Saudi Arabia, and the UAE. But governance everywhere rested on a bedrock of authoritarianism. Middle Eastern autocrats were nothing if not skilled in their craft. The Carnegie Endowment for International Peace commented that quite a few countries in the region—Algeria, Egypt, Jordan, and Morocco, among them—were 'liberalised autocracies'. Their leaders promoted reforms that appeared pluralistic, but functioned 'to preserve autocracy'. Controlled elections, divide-and-rule tactics, state interference in civil society organisations, and the obstruction of meaningful political-party systems had deeply entrenched ruling systems highly adept at thwarting democratic change. Mohamed Talbi, a Tunisian academic, commented that in contrast to the 'full autocracies' of Libya, Tunisia, Syria, and Saudi Arabia, which did not abide 'the slightest expression of dissent or pluralism,' the liberalised autocracies not only tolerated but used a strategy of 'limited, state-managed pluralism' to enhance their legitimacy and their survival. Arab rulers saw 'liberalisation' as a means of dividing the opposition and 'letting it blow off steam'. What this amounted to, said the third AHD report, was an 'acute deficit of freedom and good governance'.

The Arab world was at an historic crossroad. Caught between oppression at home and violation from abroad, Arabs were 'increasingly excluded from determining their own future'. The modern Arab state, politically, was akin to an astronomical black hole, in which the executive converted its surrounding environment 'into a setting in which nothing moves and from which nothing escapes'. Heads of state became 'the supreme leader' of everything—the executive, the council of ministers, the armed forces, the judiciary, and the public services. So-called ruling parties, where they existed, were little more than tools of the executive. Parliaments were bureaucratic adjuncts that did not represent the people. The judiciary was used 'to eliminate and tame opponents, rivals and even supporters who step out of line'. And buttressing all this was the intelligence apparatus.

Arab states varied in their embodiment of these traits. But what they had in common, said the AHD report, was power 'concentrated at the tip of the executive pyramid'. The varying margin of freedom allowed had 'no effect on the state's firm and absolute grip on power'. The survival of 'the black-hole State' lay in control and propaganda: in marginalising the elites through scare-and-promise tactics; and in striking bargains with dominant global and regional powers that reinforced the status of ruling elites against their opponents. Scenarios ranged from 'hopeful' to 'catastrophic'. Continued repression could lead to chaotic upheaval and a forcible transfer of power that might well involve armed violence and loss of life—and no certainty that successor regimes would be any more palatable. Disaster could be averted through a redistribution of power and the restoration of 'sovereignty to its rightful owners'—the people. A halfway-house scenario involved, in effect, changes being fomented by 'external forces'.

With Arab 'reform' under the spotlight, everyone, it seems, had an opinion. Recounting his experiences at the fourth assembly of the World Movement for Democracy, Amr Hamzawy, an Egyptian academic based at the Carnegie Endowment, noted that advice came flooding from every direction: a Bangladeshi minister suggested that the Arabs should emulate his country's democratisation process; an ex-Malaysian prime minister 'spoke of the need to confront despotic elites'. Eastern and Western Europeans offered high-flown, time-wasting, and depressing comments. Only two types of Arab participants, Hamzawy concluded, seemed to enjoy the conference: civil society representatives used to 'listening politely to inane advice' and Islamists, who saw others' arrogance as 'validating their own tendency for isolationism and rejecting all forms of foreign interference'.

Seemingly oblivious to the complexities of the problem, including its own dubious track record,

US promotion of Arab democratisation combined admirable idealism with cynical self-interest. It was also an admission of failure. For, in the second half of the twentieth century, the furthest thing from US thinking about the Middle East was that it should be democratised. What the US wanted, though it did not always get, was stability—stability that would keep Israel secure and would keep Middle Eastern oil flowing into American factories and its thirsty automobiles. So the US cohabited with an array of wealthy kings and unsavoury despots who kept the lid on pluralism and free expression. Saddam Hussein was no friend of Israel, but he did the job domestically—putting the plug on Islamist sentiments, providing a critical bulwark against Iran, and earning US support. Egypt's President Mubarak kept both his secular and Islamist critics reasonably well tamed, though not without occasional horrific eruptions, such as the 1997 massacre of some 60 foreign tourists near Luxor in southern Egypt. But he did enough to earn his USAID rewards.

Egypt, in fact, provided the setting for one of the most cogent explanations of the US policy turn-around. There, in mid-2005, the US secretary of state, Condoleezza Rice, confessed that, for the previous 60 years:

we were not outspoken about the need for democracy in this part of the world. In fact, at the same time that we were talking about democracy in Europe and democracy in Asia, we didn't talk about the Middle East. Things have changed. We had a very rude awakening on September 11th ... we realised that our policies to try and promote what we thought was stability in the Middle East had actually allowed a very malignant ... form of extremism to grow up underneath because people didn't have outlets for their political views.

So, the argument ran, free the Arab world from despotism, and help free America from the threat of terrorism. This would be an admirable 'win–win' for all, except of course for Middle Eastern autocrats. But they had only to look at America's record as a promoter of the democratic way to know that their world and their skins were pretty safe. A Carnegie Endowment study of America's record in democracy-building characterised 16 of the more than 200 American interventions since 1900 'as attempts at nation building through the promotion or imposition of democratic institutions desired by American policy makers'. The results were 'sobering'. Of the 16 target countries, two (Japan and West Germany) were 'unambiguous successes'; another two (Grenada and Panama) were 'considered successes'; and nation-building efforts 'failed to establish and sustain democracies' in all other targets. The overall success rate was around 25 per cent. Citing the US's relative success in Grenada (population 100,000) and Panama (around three million), the study concluded, unsurprisingly, that 'nation building generally is less challenging in small societies'. The implication for the US's approach to the Middle East was obvious. It was one thing to tell 600,000 Qataris how to run their country; another thing entirely to deliver the same message to some 75 million Egyptians. And, despite the prominence of Saudi nationals in the events of September 11, was the US really going to lay down the law to the world's richest oil state in the same way it might to impoverished Yemen?

The US faced another contradiction. Condoleezza Rice had offered an eloquent retraction of earlier American policies, which put US strategic interests ahead of the welfare of Arab citizens. But was the revamped US really all that different? Was it about principle or packaging? Did it involve genuine concern about Arab wellbeing, or awareness that its absence threatened America? There may have been a happy coincidence of interests, but was it just that? In her mid-2005 Cairo pronouncement, Rice imagined a different Middle East: a free and united Iraq, a free and democratic Palestinian state, and 'reform in great countries like Egypt'. Imagine what a different Middle East that would be, she opined. 'It will certainly not be a Middle East that produces people who want to blow up other innocent people ... That's what the United States wants to see ... for our security, [and] also because it is very close and dear to our values.' President Bush declared that, as 'long as the

Middle East remains a place of tyranny and despair and anger, it will continue to produce men and movements that threaten the safety of America and our friends'. Freedom in the United States depended 'on the success of liberty in other lands'.

This self-interested American approach should have surprised no-one. National wellbeing, quite reasonably, drives foreign policy everywhere. But there were good reasons for scepticism both about America's aims and their chances of chances. The apparent simplicity of the goal masked a raft of complex issues. What did democratic reform involve? Was democratisation the same as modernisation? How would the US deal with those who did not share its aspirations? What if democratisation led to 'Islamisation'? A high-level gathering in Egypt of civil-society activists from across the Arab region had observed that 'genuine democracy ... may differ in form and shape from one country to another due to cultural and historical variations'.

Condoleezza Rice acknowledged that democracy could not be imposed. It would never be the case, she declared, 'that democracy or a system of rules that come from the outside are going to be able to prosper inside of a country'. Yet that is exactly what drove the American approach towards 'democratising' Iraq. Rice spoke of 'everyone' having their 'own traditions ... own ways', but there remained for her a single, standard definition of democracy:

We all know a democracy when we see it. We all know that people have to have the ability to choose those who are going to govern. We all know that people have to be able to speak freely, that they have to have the ability to associate, that they have to have the ability to have a press that can inform them, that they have to have the ability to have girls and boys educated so that young women can grow up to be leaders.

Curiously absent from this list rich in 'haves' was any specific mention of religious freedom (see below).

An even more challenging break-down of the democratic way was offered by the Iranian-born American academic Majid Tehranian, who set the following criteria:

- Political democracy: popular sovereignty; universal suffrage; protection of life, liberty and the pursuit of happiness; majority rule, minority rights; fair representation and periodic elections; peaceful succession; direct voting such as referenda on critical issues; rule of law, habeas corpus, bill of rights, and responsibilities of citizenship.
- Economic democracy: protection of property; free markets; free competition; government regulation of trade and investment to ensure the absence of monopolies and fair standards in trade, exchange, competition, health, and environment.

- Social democracy: social security for the unemployed, the retired, pregnant women, and children; the provision of public health, education, and welfare.
- Cultural democracy: universal education; access to means of communication; freedom of identity, including speech, assembly, religion, language, privacy, and lifestyle.

Middle Eastern states aside, many otherwise democratic nations would struggle to meet this formidable list. One critical measure of democratisation is successive, peaceful changes of government. In the mid-1990s, no Arab state would have passed such a test. Little has changed since then, nor will it do so in the future. American dreams, badgering, military intervention, and financial inducement notwithstanding, the prospects for meaningful democratisation in the Arab Middle East, even in those states regarded most hopefully—Lebanon, Jordan, and Morocco—is slight. American rhetoric provided useful cover for those in the Arab world seeking to promote democratic reform, but American talk and muscle offered no prospect of transforming the Middle East. The administration's rhetoric, in the apt words of the prominent scholar of the Middle East Fred Halliday, lacked both analytical and moral substance, and was 'yet another example of the prevalence of one shallow policy fashion after another'. When the US administration announced, in May 2006, that it was normalising US–Libya relations, Middle Eastern autocrats must have sighed with relief. Freedom House had only recently described Libya under Muammar Gaddafi as 'one of the world's most closed and repressive societies,' where freedom of speech was 'nonexistent'. Gaddafi had improved his behaviour on the world stage, and he had reformed his behaviour towards America—but not towards his own people. Internally, democratic practice remained as comatose as ever.

In 2004, the US National Intelligence Council produced an informal discussion paper as part of its 'Middle East to 2020 project'; it offered a sobering view of the prospects for democratisation. The Middle East would continue largely as 'a story of ineffective governance ... [of] the failure of regimes to move beyond stultifying patronage politics and beyond the minimum necessary accommodations to retain power'. A civil society worthy of the name would be more apparent in 2020, but would 'continue to be overshadowed by the state above and the village below'. The paper acknowledged that there had been change over the previous half century, with opposition politics passing through secular Arab nationalist and leftist phases before 'giving way to its currently dominant Islamist colouration'. There was potential for 'still more mutation between now and 2020', but also good reason to believe that 'the current colouration will be longer lasting'.

So were Islamists and Islamism to blame for the failure of the American dream to democratise the Middle East? A leader of the Islamic Salvation Front in Algeria once declared that, 'When we are in power, there will be no more elections because God will be ruling'. This was not good news for those arguing the merits of political contestability. If anything, such a comment played into the hands of Middle East autocrats. Keen to burnish their Islamic credentials, they could also use fear of Islamist extremism to blunt both domestic and foreign criticism of the harsh nature of their rule. Denying Islamists the possibility of moving to centre stage politically through genuinely free elections inevitably fuelled tensions and violence. But this then reinforced the need for a firm, dictatorial hand at the top. The third AHD report had commented on the tendency for some regimes to style themselves as the lesser of two evils, or 'the last line of defence against fundamentalist tyranny or, even more dramatically, against chaos and the collapse of the state'. By threatening Middle Eastern autocrats, Islamism helped them justify their autocracy.

Islamists posed a problem, but did Islam itself? Francis Fukuyma — hardly a promoter of Muslim interests — wrote nonetheless that the idea that the problem stemmed 'from Islam itself as a religion seems to me extremely unlikely. All of the world's major religious systems are highly complex. Christianity was once …

used to justify slavery and hierarchy; now we see it is
as supportive of modern democracy.' Those who argued
that the indivisibility of God and state within Islam
posed an insuperable problem for democratic practice
overlooked the fact that democracy had generally
worked well in Malaysia, had made an important
comeback in Indonesia—the world's largest Muslim
nation—and continued to function effectively in India,
home to the world's third-largest Muslim population
after Indonesia and Pakistan. Ironically, the same God
seemed to directing Islamists, moderate Muslims, Jews,
and Christians. George Bush, for example, asserted that
God told him to 'go and end the tyranny in Iraq. And I
did.' The then British prime minister, Tony Blair, though
more circumspect about the Almighty's involvement in
his Middle Eastern decision-making, acknowledged that
God would judge his decision to send troops to Iraq.

A true irony, and tragedy, of Middle Eastern
democratisation is the fact that one of its few successes
became one it its greatest setbacks. At American urging,
the one Arab 'Head of State' who allowed genuinely free
elections, in early 2006, was the Palestinian president,
Mahmud Abbas. Yet the US and Israel, in particular,
disowned the result—not because the electoral process
was flawed, but because it delivered the 'wrong result'
in the form of an Islamist Hamas government. Here
was a salutary lesson to Middle Eastern autocrats of
the dangers of the democratic process, and further

justification for resisting it—justification that the US could hardly disown, given its own reaction to Hamas' victory. Some commentators argued that the Palestinian parliament would, in fact, 'tame' Hamas. The US and Israelis, in particular, were not prepared to take the risk of such on-the-job training. In spurning the free choice of the Palestinian people, they endorsed the 'Islam as threat' excuse for dictators across the Arab world.

One of the hurdles faced by Middle Eastern liberal reformers was the apparent linkage between democracy and 'modernisation'. Fouad Ajami, the Lebanese-born American academic and Bush administration darling, wrote that the force of 'a new American endeavour in Iraq and in neighbouring Arab lands should be modernising the Arab world'. Consider the implications of this against the *Encyclopaedia Britannica's* definition of modernisation as a process of secularisation that 'systematically displaces religious institutions, beliefs and practices, substituting for them those of reason and science'. Could there ever have been any real hope for Middle East democratisation if this meant disowning the religious heart of Arabism? True, only around 25 per cent of the world's 1.3 billion Muslims actually live in the Middle East, and Muslims elsewhere had been able to bridge the divide between religion and democratic modernism. The world's two largest Muslims nations—Indonesia and Pakistan—had both elected female heads of government. But, with the failure of Arab regionalism and socialism, there should have been no surprise at the re-emergence of Islamism as the 'natural' political colouration of Arab politics. And this world-view, in its most ardent form, saw the problems of the Middle East as stemming not from too little but, rather, too much modernisation.

Criticising the Islam-is-the-problem argument, *The Economist* noted that, while 'many Islamists' insisted that God alone could make law,' this remained a minority view in the world of Islam, where democracy had put down powerful roots in countries as far apart as Turkey and Indonesia. There was no 'obvious reason why the Arab world must remain an exception'. Yet, far into the future, the Arab world is likely to be precisely that. Part of the easy explanation is to blame American tactical failures, inconsistency, and insincerity. Israel, too, readily becomes part of the excuse — because of its very existence, because of the way it behaves, and because it is America's closest friend in the Middle East. As with so many aspects of the conflict between Jew and Arab, a glib rationale does not amount to an explanation. If anything, Israel provides an uncomfortable model for the Arab world: a society bursting with friction between the modern and the traditional, between secular and religious elements, but where the rules of the democratic game are understood and genuinely implemented, and where there have been peaceful changes of government.

The problem was not Islam *per se*, but the heady mix of Islam and Arabism, and the way that religion lay at

the heart of Arab identity. There is no better illustration
of this—and of the toxic conflict between Islamic
precept, modernisation, and democratic reform—than
the issue of religious freedom and apostasy. In the Arab
world, apostasy remains nominally punishable by death
in countries such as Saudi Arabia, Qatar, Yemen, Sudan,
and Mauritania. In the broader Islamic world, the same
penalty is applied in Afghanistan and Iran. In Pakistan,
blasphemy is a capital offence. Could any of these states
ever be accepted as moving towards genuine democracy
while they deny one of its most fundamental tenets:
religious freedom of choice? In one of his post-9/11
declarations, president Bush cited equal justice and
religious tolerance as one of the mainstays of the 'single
surviving model of human progress' that America was
determined to pursue. The hypocrisy is breathtaking.
Can we really imagine the US telling the Saudis, for
example, that they must implement freedom of religion,
and that Saudi citizens—automatically Muslims at
birth—must not be beheaded because they opt for
another religion, or indeed for none at all?

Adam Garfinkle, editor of *American Interest* magazine
and a former speechwriter for the US secretary of state,
has written that there were few genuine democracies in
the Muslim world, 'and none in the Arab world'. This, he
argued, was 'no coincidence'. In differing degrees, Arab
societies lacked three prerequisites for democracy: the
belief that the source of political authority was intrinsic

to society; a concept of majority rule; and acceptance that all citizens are equal before the law. Without the first, the idea of pluralism — and the legitimacy of a 'loyal opposition' — could not exist. Without the second, the idea of elections as a means to form a government was 'incomprehensible'. Without the third, 'a polity can be neither free nor liberal as those terms are understood in the West'. Dealing with the 'pathologies of the Arab world,' Garfinkle added, was one of the 'greatest challenges of our time'.

Yet those 'pathologies' might well have reflected the coincidence of interests between Arab autocrats and Western governments. Both paid lip-service to democracy, but neither really wanted it. They had, among other uncomfortable examples of a growing Islamist tide, the experience of Algeria in the 1990s — when the army intervened to stop the Islamic Salvation Front's democratic rise to power — and the 'surprise' election of a Hamas government by the Palestinians in 2006. 'Democracy' became a useful catch-cry and little more. Genuine democracy, implemented across the region, would have turned the Middle East on its head. Instead, governments across the Arab Middle East held out to Islamists and others the prospect of political involvement, determined to ensure that democratisation remained a myth. Who really cared, apart from small pockets of ineffectual and often cowed liberals, and larger numbers of Islamists intent on replacing autocratic fundamentalism with their own?

The Egyptian academic Amr Hamzawy wrote that while 'moderate Islamists' continued to call for the establishment of Islamic states across the region, this was increasingly a matter of 'symbolic language'. He argued that a new consensus had emerged among Islamists in countries such as Jordan, Yemen, and Egypt, accepting that the 'utopia of the Islamic state' could best be realised in the contemporary Arab world by 'adhering in each country to the principles of democracy, the rule of law, and human rights'. If this were true, moderate Islamists had a much greater commitment to democratic reform than the region's authoritarian rulers.

The autocrats continued to exercise a stranglehold on power, not without some gestures towards their opponents and not without some uncomfortable moments. But they stayed on top, ensuring that 'democratic reform' remained more a theatrical production than a reality. What accounted for the success of the autocrats? In the oil-rich states, the answer had a lot to do with the mostly unspoken pact between the rulers and the ruled that the former, after taking their considerable share of national revenues, would dole out the rest in ways that would provide a largely work-free and tax-free existence for the broader population. The 2004 US National Intelligence Council discussion paper commented that oil funded huge patronage systems which turned 'workers, professionals, intellectuals, businesspeople into dependents' of the state. The unhealthy collusion between commerce and autocracy, the fusion of political and economic power by state elites, 'only magnified the risk of reform'. Oil kept regimes afloat. It provided copious walking-around money. High oil prices weakened pressure for both political and economic change. The connection between taxation and representation was reversed. The recompense for being politically neutered was the bounty of the welfare state.

The Council on Foreign Relations (CFR) had noted that, in some countries, the majority of people might be content with the status quo. Dubai's citizens, for example, enjoyed 'significant prosperity and stability without democracy'. In oil-rich countries, a shift towards more open, transparent economies would threaten the elites. In non-oil states, quaintly termed the 'labour-abundant countries', there was concern that a freeing up of the economy would 'threaten social cohesion' as the reduction of subsidies and privatisation proceeded. Economic growth, said the CFR, was 'crucial for the durability of democracies', but of itself did 'not directly cause democracy'. Singapore provides a splendid example of this truism—in 2005 it had the world's seventh-highest per-capita income, yet was still rated by Freedom House as still only 'partly free'.

With taxation low, a key incentive for citizens' concerns about government was effectively removed. In

2002, taxes accounted for 17 per cent of gross domestic product in non-oil Arab countries, and 5 per cent in the oil states. This compared to around 23 per cent in Germany, 24 per cent in Italy, and 28 per cent in the United Kingdom. Moreover, in Arab countries the majority of tax receipts were indirect and hidden. The lack of a clear, observable link between tax payments and the public purse did little to promote the cause of accountability. No wonder the AHD report observed that taxes provided 'no major stimulus for Arab citizens to call the government to account for what it does with their money'.

Arab rulers, who had every reason to fear the democratisation of political and economic power, used the financial and institutional authority of the state to good effect to buy off and co-opt enemies and potential enemies, who in any case were often deeply fragmented. Astute 'reformers', such as Egypt's President Mubarak, also realised the benefits of a blossoming of civil-society groupings. The British-based academic Katerina Dalacoura commented that 'liberalised autocracies' not only permitted but actually promoted the growth of non-government or quasi-government organisations. These provided many state services while the government retained 'ultimate control', and the opposition was further fragmented. The rulers could point to the existence of thousands of organisations as demonstrating their commitment to reform and liberalisation. In practice, this meant very little. Leakage of real power from the executive and the government political party remained minimal, and democracy stayed a theatrical production. There was, of course, one instance where a non-government grouping, Hamas, established sufficiently deep roots in society to bring it to power via a democratic election. For autocratic Arab rulers and the US (and Israel), the lesson from this was clear: avoid genuine expressions of popular feeling unless the right result can be guaranteed.

The 2004 AHD report asked why Arabs enjoyed 'so little freedom'. What had led Arab democratic institutions, even where they existed, to lose their original purpose? The report debunked the idea of despotism as an inherent characteristic of 'the East' and 'Eastern civilisation', or that Arabs and Muslims were not capable of being democrats because of their Arabness or the nature of Islam. The explanation, the report said, lay in the convergence of political, social, and economic factors. These had suppressed or eliminated social and political actors 'capable of turning the crisis of authoritarian and totalitarian regimes to their advantage'. These factors also had 'a far-reaching impact on attitudes of the major powers towards freedom in the Arab region'. What this boiled down to was the West's continuing need for Middle Eastern oil, and its vested interest in supporting Israel.

The West could easily be blamed for the Middle

East's political, economic, and social woes. But pointing the finger outward only delayed the need to point it inward. Arab dictators, the Tunisian historian Mohamad Talbi wrote, had 'succeeded in hypnotising their people'. History did not provide fertile ground for optimism about the democratic prospect. Political reforms seemed 'likely only to repeat the cycle of repression and liberalisation, or, in some cases, to enlarge the ranks of liberalised autocracies'. The system was 'not angelic' and 'not run by choir boys'. But 'in the Arab world' it was 'a tradition'.

Others, too, saw something in Arab culture that made it resistant to democratisation. Fukuyama described this as 'a cultural obstacle ... not related to religion, such as the survival of tribalism'. Denying that despotism was an inherent characteristic in the Middle East, the AHD report pointed the finger at 'clannism'—the 'enemy of personal independence, intellectual daring, and the flowering of a unique and authentic human entity'. Clannism flourished, and its negative impact on freedom and society became stronger, 'wherever civil or political institutions that protect rights and freedoms' were absent. Without institutional support, individuals sought refuge in narrow loyalties that provided security and protection. Clannism's function was 'the reproduction of control in Arab societies'. Fred Halliday also emphasised the power of the clan and of the family. The families of rulers, not politicians, he wrote, held power, and took 'their percentage of state money ... conventionally it can be assumed that around one-third of all state revenues is pocketed by the ruler and his relatives and close associates'. This, not the corruption of politicians as such, was 'the core malaise' of Middle Eastern states.

Middle Eastern rulers faced a simple question. Would democracy cost them more — politically and financially — than it might conceivably benefit them? The answer overwhelmingly was yes, particularly as the main beneficiary might well be their sometimes-vehement Islamist opponents, not the small, often-fragmented proponents of liberalism in their societies. The task, then, was to release political pressure while resisting the institutional or social changes that might destroy their positions of unique wealth and privilege. Democracy, as the West liked to portray it, never had a chance.

To this intrinsic explanation for democracy's failure in the Middle East we must add an extrinsic one: the role of the US and its supporters. The US studiously avoided suggesting that democracy could be imposed, while working energetically in Iraq to prove that it could. This, undoubtedly, caused alarm among Arab autocrats, who feared that they might be next on the list. In reality, they had little to worry about. One Iraqi Shia offered the pithy comment that the country had simply changed rule by a dictator to rule by clowns. The Iraqi quagmire and the lesson of Hamas' win in the 2006 Palestinian election quickly dulled America's appetite for genuine democratic reform. And as the US, urged on by Israel, turned its attention to the threat—real or otherwise—posed by Iran, it simply could not afford further alienation of its erstwhile Arab partners. The Bush administration performed a *mea culpa* for past American policies, apologising for its preparedness to sacrifice democratic values for the sake of authoritarian stability. But, despite the shock of 9/11 and the spotlight this turned on Saudi Arabia, the dangers of trying to democratise the Middle East quickly became apparent. The former CIA officer Robert Baer suggested that Washington's answer for Saudi Arabia, 'apart from repeating that nothing is wrong', was to suggest that

> a little democracy will cure everything. Talk the royal family into ceding at least part of its authority; support the reform-minded princes; set up a model parliament; co-opt the firebrands with a cabinet position or two, a minor political party, and some outright bribery; send Jimmy Carter in to monitor the first election; and in a few generations Riyadh will be Ankara, maybe even London ... It's utter nonsense, of course. If an election were held in Saudi Arabia today, if anyone who wanted to could run for the office of president, and if people could vote with their hearts without fear of having their heads cut off afterward in Chop-Chop Square, Osama bin Laden would be elected in a landslide—not because the Saudi people want to wash

their hands in the blood of the dead of September 11, but simply because bin Laden has dared to do what even the mighty United States of America won't do: stand up to the thieves who rule the country.

This was not an encouraging picture for anyone wanting peaceful, democratic change.

The US and its friends in the West viewed democracy as a prophylactic against extremism, especially the Islamist variety. The war on terror was converted into the war for democratisation of the Middle East: it would drain the swamp, reducing if not eliminating the causes of anger and frustration which lay behind some, though by no means all, terrorism. But, if anything, the war on terrorism set back the cause of democratisation: Iraq descended into sectarian strife, in which the biggest winners were al-Qaeda and Iran. True, the 'surge' in US troops in Iraq in 2007–08 reduced the death rate, at least temporarily. Yet, as of late 2008 an average of 10 Iraqi security force personnel and civilians were being or killed *daily*. In an attempt to dissuade them from emigrating, Iraq's doctors are now allowed to carry guns.

The war on terror made the Middle East more, not less, authoritarian. Some Islamists appeared willing to work within the system, especially if they knew that state institutions had the will and the power to curb them (Turkey being the clearest example). But democratisation also offered a path to power for Islamists denied a legitimate place in Arab politics over many years — not because they lacked popular support, but because their ideas were unacceptable to US-aligned regimes. Democratisation became a Pandora's box, out of which the Islamists were first to jump. So the lid was quickly levered back into place. Even Fouad Ajami recanted, conceding that Iraq was not going to become 'America's showcase' in the Islamic world and that the US had 'returned to our accommodation with the established order of power in the Arab world'.

In the first years of the twentieth century, there was no such thing as an independent Arab state; in the early years of the twenty-first century, there were 21 of them. To this total, we need to add the Palestinian areas of the Gaza Strip and the West Bank, although their prospects for meaningful statehood have evaporated. The inhabitants of these states, in Mohammad Talbi's estimation, were 'colonised natives' rather than 'citizens'. At the turn of the twenty-first century, he wrote, if 'the criterion of a democracy is the turnover of political power by peaceful means, that is elections considered free, fair, perfectly transparent, and indisputably and irrefutably incontestable — in a word, honest — then not a single Arab country is democratic today'.

As this book was being written, the only government in the Arab world elected without American troops breathing down voters' necks — the Hamas-led

government in the Palestinian areas—was shunned
by the US and Europe. Clearly, the play had not run
to script. Middle Eastern democratisation was electing
illiberal rather than liberal forces, increasing rather than
diminishing the prospect for future conflict. After the
American invasion of Iraq and the realisation that some
Iraqis, and their unsavoury foreign accomplices, might
actually resist it, Lt General William Wallace, commander
of V Corps, noted: 'The enemy we're fighting is a bit
different from the one we war-gamed against'. At least
there had been an attempt, no matter how misplaced,
to imagine the military foe. When it came to remaking
the Middle East politically, ideological fixation and
ignorance proved to be a lethal combination. As they
retreated into their crusader-like military redoubts
in Iraq, and as they rewarded Libya—the antithesis
of democratic practice—with full normalisation of
relations, Americans must have known that the game
was over. Democratisation had proved a mirage: forever
on the horizon, but never any closer.

CHAPTER THREE

Whose Islam is It?

Imagine for a moment that the once seemingly inexhaustible supply of Middle Eastern oil was now gone. That the Sahara—thanks to climate change—had become a lush, tropical expanse. That the camel, for so long a symbol in Western minds of the timeless, enigmatic qualities of the Arab world, was now extinct (a victim, perhaps, of climatically induced footrot). What would remain to draw us to the region, to ponder its place in our lives? The answer lies readily to hand. For the region's potent religious legacy—the three great monotheistic religions—drives the beliefs and actions of half of all humankind in all the continents of the globe. Whatever the future of oil, of deserts, and camels, that spiritual reality will live on.

In the Arab world, the main if not exclusive vehicle for this legacy will remain Islam. Like its fellow religions of the book, Judaism and Christianity, it is a religion of uncertainties, of contrary interpretations, reinterpretations, and misinterpretations. It underpins high human ideals, yet is also used as cover by some adherents for outrageous actions. At times, the tensions within Islam seem even greater than those between it and the world beyond. Despite this, perhaps because of it, Islam will assume an even greater prominence in the Arab Middle East. For the harsh reality is that the region's other 'gods' have all failed. Those of Arab nationalism and regionalism, of socialism and democracy, belong either to an inglorious past or seem dim specks on an uncertain future horizon. What is left other than the certainty of an idea that, more than any other, shaped a singular Arab identity, that fed Arab self-assurance and a sense of superiority over its rival 'religions of the Book'? Islam, like no other force, will go on shaping lives and politics, explaining the past, and charting the future. In the Arab Middle East, it is literally the last idea standing.

But move from that broad comment to the specifics, and we quickly enter a terminological minefield. Labels such as Islamists, Islamo-fascists, jihadists, Islamic extremists, militants, radicals, fundamentalists (a term derived from American Protestantism), moderates, and reformers often pepper conversations and commentaries as if the meaning is self-evident and self-contained. One typology of Muslims published by the Rand Corporation plotted them from 'radical fundamentalists, scriptural fundamentalists, conservative traditionalists, reformists and traditionalists to modernists, mainstream secularists, and radical secularists'. Non-Muslims, in particular, often seem to view 'Islamism' as inherently violent and dangerous: it is the 'ism' of threat, as in communism, rather than that of belief, as, for example, in Judaism. Islamism might put religion at the heart of human existence, but does that make Islamists violent by definition? Then there is the notion that radical Islam grows largely from migration and 'detribalisation'. In turn, this is pitted against the claim of Islam's inherently warlike nature. The Bush administration's Iraq adventure was later explained by the need to take on Islamic extremists on their home ground. Yet invading this home ground clearly was a major factor in creating such 'extremism', involving as it does an often deadly mix of religion, nationalism, and opportunism.

An International Crisis Group report, *Understanding Islamism*, observed that Islamism or Islamic activism, the two being synonymous, had 'a number of very different streams, only a few of them violent and only a small minority justifying a confrontational approach'. The report usefully divided Sunni Islamism into three main streams:

- Political — exemplified by the Muslim Brotherhood in Egypt and its offshoots in Algeria, Jordan, the Palestinian areas, Syria, and elsewhere, and 'locally rooted movements' such as the Justice and Development Party in Turkey, and the Party for Justice and Development in Morocco. Having generally accepted the nation state, their main purpose was to attain political power at the national level. They eschewed violence except under foreign occupation (the Muslim Brotherhood, for example, continuing to support Hamas violence against Israeli occupation);

- Missionary—for whom the overriding objective was not political power but the preservation of Muslim identity and Islam against the forces of unbelief; and
- Jihadi—involving three sorts of armed struggle: against Muslim regimes considered to be impious; irredentists fighting to redeem land ruled by non-Muslims or under occupation; and a global struggle against the West.

Political Islamists made an issue of Muslim misgovernment and social injustice, and gave priority to reform through political action; missionary Islamists focused on the corruption of Islamic values; and Jihadi Islamists were driven by what they portrayed as 'the oppressive weight of non-Muslim political and military power in the Islamic world'.

It is quite possible to imagine activists migrating between different streams to pursue changing ambitions. In Egypt, for example, the still legally proscribed Muslim Brotherhood has formally renounced violence. Yet it ran 130 'independent' candidates in the 2005 elections, winning 88 of the 454 seats in the Peoples' Assembly. This success disconcerted the Mubarak regime, despite its own stranglehold on power. For very different reasons, it also upset al-Qaeda, which portrayed the brotherhood as having sold out. Ayman al-Zawahiri, the Egyptian-born doctor widely regarded as Osama bin Laden's deputy, accused the brotherhood of being a tool of US 'democratisation' policy(!). Abu Musab al-Zarqawi, the Jordanian-born terrorist who became the leading al-Qaeda figure in Iraq, charged that the brotherhood had put elections ahead of jihad: a 'strategy which is a losing one for Sunnis'.

The political–missionary–jihadi framework may well be permeable, but it usefully focuses attention on three important factors: goals; methodology; and the distinction between Islamo-nationalism, involving Muslim rule within the nation state, and Islamo-internationalism, which demands Muslim rule within a much more broadly and often vaguely defined geographic area.

If there is confusion, distortion, and disinformation in the non-Muslim world about Islam and its followers, the Muslim world brims with its own internal tensions. The ideal of Muslim unity has fallen prey to the reality of fissures between Arab Muslims themselves and between them and non-Arab Muslims. The Arab Middle East of the seventh century gave Islam to the world; that religion remains a, perhaps *the*, defining characteristic of Arab identity. Some 95 per cent of Arabs are Muslim. But the region and the belief are no longer synonymous—only one-quarter of the world's 1.3 billion Muslims are Arab. Indeed, some Muslims outside the Middle East see Arabness as a burden, to be held at arms' length. But they cannot avoid the reality that Islam's heart, like that of Judaism and Christianity, beats in the Middle East—in Mecca, Medina, and Jerusalem. The battle for Islam's soul is a Middle Eastern one, an Arab one. Certainly, it has broader resonances—from Nigeria to Chechnya, from Afghanistan to Indonesia. But Muslim grievances wherever are refracted through the prism of the Middle East; of Jewish dispossession of the Palestinians; of non-Muslim troops treading Muslim soil as occupiers of Islamic lands; and of governments outside the region conniving with those within regarded by their domestic critics as venal and un-Islamic, if not anti-Islamic.

Yet no more than any other broad region does the Arab Middle East have a single identity. Its recent and longer-term history reflects the pull of competing national, regional, and philosophical forces. A 2004 survey conducted jointly by the Anwar Sadat Chair for Peace and Development at the University of Maryland and Zogby International (a major US pollster) gave respondents in Jordan, Lebanon, Morocco, Saudi Arabia, Egypt, and the United Arab Emirates (UAE) five options for their primary identity: as citizens of their country; as Arabs; as Muslims; as international citizens;

and as not sure. The same options were offered for
their secondary identity. The number of respondents
identifying themselves primarily as Muslims was highest
in the UAE (66 per cent) and Saudi Arabia (56 per cent),
followed by Morocco (48 per cent) and Jordan (33 per
cent). Lebanese and Egyptians identified themselves
primarily as citizens of their own country (77 per cent
and 59 per cent, respectively). Most secondary identities
were Arab, although Moroccan respondents identified
themselves as Moroccans ahead of Arabs (32 per cent
and 28 per cent respectively). Egyptian identity tilted
slightly toward Islam (37 per cent), ahead of Arab (35
per cent).

Respondents were asked also about religion and
politics, and the role of the clergy in political life. Only
28 per cent of Lebanese and 33 per cent of Moroccan
respondents wanted the clergy to play a greater role,
against 42 per cent in Jordan, 45 per cent in the UAE,
47 per cent in Egypt, and 48 per cent in Saudi Arabia.
Nearly 20 per cent of respondents in Jordan, Morocco,
and Lebanon felt that the clergy played too much of
a role, against less than 5 per cent in Saudi Arabia or
the UAE. Curiously, all respondents felt that the need
for religious involvement in Arab states as a whole was
higher than it was in their own country.

Underlining these fractured self-identities is the great
divide within Islam between and Shia and Sunni, driven
essentially by the question of whether succession to the

Prophet should be determined by bloodline (the Shia) or merely exemplary behaviour (the Sunnis). The picture is greatly complicated by non-Arab Iran's centrality in the Shia world, and the questions this raises of the pull of 'foreign' powers and divided loyalties. The Iranian-born American academic Sayyed Vali Nasr argued in *The Shia Revival* that Iraqi Shia were distancing themselves from Arab nationalism, defining themselves instead in terms of state nationalism (as Iraqis) and religion (as Shia). The Shia revival, he wrote, meant anchoring Shia interests in national identities. Iraqi Shia had joined the new security forces in droves, the new state was their state, and they had much to gain. Extremist Sunni attacks on the police and security forces were not just or even primarily aimed at the American occupation, but at impeding 'the emergence of the Shia-dominated nation'.

Beneath this sometimes bloody theological schism lies a broader angst within Islam, the reality of a longstanding Middle Eastern and Arab malaise: of Muslim impotence (Sunni and Shia) in the face of others' ambitions and power. Against the backdrop of the Arab world succumbing to the non-Muslim Christian invader during the period of European colonial domination for Middle Eastern Muslims — Sunnis in particular — the twentieth century often must have seemed a long journey of humiliations: the abolition of the caliphate in 1922 by a new-found Turkish secularism jealously guarded by the military; the creation of Israel on

Palestinian Arab and Muslim territory; and the triumph of this foreign implant over Arab leaders, armies, and peoples. The cause of Palestine lies at the heart of al-Qaeda's portrayal of the West's 'crusade' against Islam, and resonates throughout the Muslim world.

In *Islam vs. Islamism*, the Canadian academic Peter Demant wrote that what emerged from decades of Arab defeat, self-doubt, and the failures of state and region was an Arab world in crisis, one that created 'space for an anti-modern, anti-secular, and anti-Western mentality; space for religious fundamentalism'. Islam carried a message of worldly and spiritual supremacy over Christianity and Judaism. Yet these other 'Peoples of the Book' had outflanked and outfought Middle Eastern Muslims with seeming ease. Demant argued that, for the Islamic world, colonisation meant not just the loss of political and military control, but also the humiliation of a lifestyle that viewed itself 'as intrinsically superior to any other'. Of all the world's ancient centres of civilisation, the Islamic world was 'the most backward, fragmented, repressive, and anti-egalitarian, and—despite all verbal expressions of Islamic solidarity—anything but fraternal'. Of all regions once controlled by the West, nowhere were the 'questions of cultural penetration and alienation higher on the agenda than in the Islamic world'.

Yet, in adding another layer to Muslim humiliation, Israel's birth also gave a potent tool to Islamic extremists: the gift of grievance. To this 'gift' we should add two others. The first is globalisation. Its impact, especially the seemingly all-pervasive influence of 'Western values', has affected Muslim and non-Muslim alike. But the collective interpretation of the past by many Arab Muslims undoubtedly sharpened the drowning feeling. The American academic Patricia Crone wrote that, wherever they live, Muslims 'are ruled by the West ... not just politically but also socially and culturally. Wherever they look, they are being invaded by so-called Western values, in the form of giant billboards advertising self-indulgence, semi-pornographic films, liquor, pop music, fat tourists in indecent clothes and funny hats, and politicians lecturing people about the virtues of democracy'.

Globalisation, of course, has gone hand-in-hand with modernisation. The former may well sharpen the grievances of some Muslims; the latter often offers them ready access to the tools of protest, violent and non-violent. They may seek a return to past Islamic glories, and turn their back on the modern world. But it is barely a half-turn. They may argue that the problems of the Arab world are not a lack but rather an excess of modernity. But they rely on the tools of modernisation — the Internet, the mobile phone, the Kalashnikov rifle, the roadside bomb. To be anti-modern is definitely not to be anti-modern. The Taliban may have been happy to stage public 'executions' of television sets. In Iran, however, Ayatollah Khomeini and his mullahtocracy discovered that, far from being the previously reviled 'Box of Satan', television offered an effective propaganda medium.

The second gift to Islamic extremists began with the US-led invasion of Iraq in 2003. Whatever his egregious ways, the late, unlamented Saddam Hussein used Islam for his own purposes, but kept Islamic extremism on a tight leash. Herbert Meyer, a one-time vice-chairman of the CIA's National Intelligence Council, has written that the underlying strategy behind the war in Iraq was to remove Islamic radicals from power and to 'give the moderates a chance. Our hope is that, over time, the moderates will find a way to bring Islam forward into the 21st century'. The idea is laughable, both in describing the situation in Iraq prior to the invasion—Saddam Hussein's rule rested on dictatorship, brutality, *and* modernisation—and its outcome. Even Meyer seemed to have second thoughts, noting that it was possible 'we're asking too much of Islam all at once. We're trying to jolt them from the 7th century to the 21st century all at once, which may be further than they can go'.

In the same article, Meyer pointed an accusing finger at Iran, conveniently ignoring the fact that US policy in Iraq achieved the extraordinary double of religious radicalisation of its domestic politics and the empowerment of Iran. Supporters of the invasion now claim that the unintended consequence of the invasion and occupation—Iraq as a magnet for Islamic extremists—is, in fact, a plus. They can be bottled up there and disposed of. But Iraq has proved much more of a maternity ward than a mortuary for Islamic extremists. It will go on doing so. We need look no further than the official US national-intelligence estimate in April 2006 that the Iraq conflict had 'become the *cause celebre* for jihadists, breeding a deep resentment of US involvement in the Muslim world and cultivating supporters for the global jihadist movement'. Other security officials have described Iraq as the 'university of terror', where destructive skills are honed as they were against the Soviet Union in Afghanistan. The Arab world, primarily Saudi Arabia and Egypt, supplies the bulk of the students. In the world of extremist Sunni Islam, the uncorking of Shia power in Iraq was a disaster. America and its allies might have portrayed the battle as one between freedom and oppression, but on the ground it quickly morphed into the historically and politically primed battle between the 'two halves' of Islam.

This leads to the question of Islamic violence and terrorism. The latter is defined here as the deliberate targeting of civilians, preferably on a large scale, to create both panic and political fall-out. It is a highly effective tool, often the weapon of the weak in one-sided conflicts, and it takes on a particularly chilling and gruesome quality when the perpetrator(s) set out to die alongside their victims. Several points should be emphasised about 'Islamic' violence and (especially suicide) terrorism. The first is that Islam, as Peter Demant has argued, 'is neither more violent than other religions nor does it predispose its followers to fanaticism ... Much violence is committed by Muslims ... misrepresentation is also rife. Other religions have not been less cruel than Islam'.

Those professing Christianity, not Islam, produced the Holocaust. Mass killings in Cambodia in the 1970s and in Rwanda in the 1990s had nothing to do with Islam. There is, of course, a long and disputed history of inter-faith violence between Muslim, Jew, and Christian. All have behaved badly on occasion; on occasion, all have behaved nobly. When Pope Urban II exalted the Christian faithful to recover Jerusalem from Muslim hands in late 1095, he urged them to sew a cross on their clothing, and promised heavenly rewards to all who fell in Christendom's holy quest. When the crusaders finally captured Jerusalem in mid-1099, they slaughtered virtually every Muslim and Jew, including women and children. This was a stark contrast indeed with Saladin's behaviour a century later, when he led a successful Muslim counterattack on Jerusalem, and merely imposed a ransom on non-Muslims. But all this really tells us is about Saladin: it hardly amounts to a permanent reflection on Islam, one way or another, anymore than the Holocaust should remain an indictment on all things German.

In recent times, the worst 'Islamic' violence has been Muslim against Muslim, led by Hafez al-Assad in Syria and Saddam Hussein in Iraq. Both acted primarily to crush Islamist challenges. The Syrian military's attack against the town of Hama in 1982 to quell a revolt by the Muslim Brotherhood killed at least 10,000 and possibly as many as 40,000; Saddam Hussein's war against revolutionary Iran, and his own Shia and Kurdish populations, left hundreds of thousands of Iraqis dead. In Sudan, the primarily Muslim-on-Muslim conflict in Darfur has left nearly half a million people dead, and has displaced upwards of two million more.

These appalling statistics do not point to the inherently violent nature of Islam. Yet, writing in the *Middle East Quarterly*, Daniel Mandel and Asaf Romirowsky set out to 'unmask' those on the Council on Foreign Relations who, they alleged, downplayed the threats from the Muslim Middle East. They cited State Department statistics showing that between 1961 and 2003, terrorists killed 3,776 Americans. 'Of that number, Muslim terrorist groups killed all but some two hundred.' As it happens, some 3000 of the total number were killed on 11 September 2001, meaning that the remaining 600-or-so victims of specifically Islamic violence lost their lives over 42 years. This does not make them any less victims, nor their deaths any more justifiable. But an average of 15 victims per year does bring a different perspective to bear. Some 16,000 Americans are murdered annually, mainly by their fellow citizens armed with guns, knives, and other weapons.

Around 800 of the total are killed with 'blunt objects' such as hammers, golf clubs, and baseball bats (which figure in nearly 30 per cent of all violent crime). The official crime statistics make it clear that Americans are at more risk from sporting paraphernalia than they are from Muslim terrorists.

There is another, important, point. Until the American-led invasion of Iraq, a majority of suicide killings were not carried out by Muslims. In his important study, *Dying to Win: the strategic logic of suicide terrorism*, Robert Pape compiled a database of every suicide attack around the globe between 1980 and 2003, a total of 315. The data showed there was little connection between suicide terrorism and Islamic extremism, or indeed with any of the world's religions. The leading practitioners of suicide terrorism were the Tamil Tigers in Sri Lanka, who committed 76 of the 315 incidents, more than the figure for Hamas. The figure for Islamic suicide terrorism will certainly require revision in the light of the carnage in Iraq since 2003, carried out by Sunni and Shia extremists. But Pape's observation that nearly all suicide terrorist attacks had the specific 'secular and strategic goal' of compelling modern democracies to withdraw military forces from territory that the terrorists 'considered to be their homeland' seems tailor-made for Iraq. So, too, is his comment that religion rarely was the root cause, but was often used as a recruitment tool in the service of the broader strategic objective. Pape wrote that suicide terrorism had become the most deadly form of terrorism. It accounted for just 3 per cent of all terrorist attacks between 1980 and 2003, yet produced 48 per cent of all casualties.

The non-Muslim world certainly needs a sharper appreciation of Islam's internal contest. It needs also to recognise its own failings of thought and action. Yet 'Islam' does have a problem, of both perception and reality: the ambitions of its fanatical adherents bring them into violent contact with others. The vast majority of their victims are Muslim, the starkest comparison being between Iraq and Israel. More Iraqi Muslims have been killed in suicide terror attacks in the past half-decade than Israelis have been killed by suicide terrorists in the 60 years of their country's modern existence. Muslim theologians face a considerable dilemma in trying to justify both suicide terrorism and the mass killing of other Muslims. On suicide terrorism, the Koran appears to be unambiguous: 'Do not kill yourself; for surely God has been merciful to you'. Proclaiming a suicide bomber as a 'martyr' is a dubious way of getting around the problem, given that martyrs traditionally die gallantly at the hands of others, not by blowing themselves to pieces.

Getting around Koranic proscription on the killing of civilians, especially women and children, also demands mental gymnastics. One of the best examples of this is a 2003 'Treatise on the Law of the Use of Weapons of Mass Destruction Against the Unbelievers' written by

Saudi dissident Sheik Nasir bin Hamad al-Fahd. Al-Fahd argued that, with the world's Muslims under attack and too weak to defend themselves against unbelievers through conventional military means, they had no other choice, even if they had to kill 'without exception'. This leads us, inexorably, to al-Qaeda. The prominent British historian and writer William Dalrymple has rightly decried the intellectual paucity of much debate about the organisation. It is all too easy to caricature it as driven by a primitive religious fanaticism which hates all that the West supposedly stands for. In fact, many of its operatives tend to be well-educated and middle class. They have no great knowledge of, nor interest in, the finer points of Islam and, indeed, display a general disdain for what Dalrymple termed the 'nit-picking juridical approach' of the *ulama* (Muslim clergy).

Other Muslims might decry Islam's dilemmas. Al-Qaedists portray themselves as acting to resolve them. Often, their aims are political as much as theological—although, given the holistic world-view of the jihadi stream into which al-Qaeda obviously falls, such a distinction seems redundant. As for Muslim victims of al-Qaeda inspired violence, in answer to questions posted on an al-Qaeda website in late 2007 and early 2008, Ayman al-Zawahiri, al-Qaeda's strategic brain, declared: 'We haven't killed the innocents; not in Baghdad, nor in Morocco, nor in Algeria, nor anywhere else.' If any 'innocent' had been killed this was either 'unintentional error, or out of necessity as in cases of *al-Tatarrus*', the latter invoking a fatwa that sanctions the killing of Muslims being used as human shields by an enemy.

Osama bin Laden's stated aim is the restoration of the Islamic caliphate, abolished in the 1920s by the ardently secularist Turkish nationalist Kemal Ataturk, following the collapse of Ottoman rule, Islam's last great empire. For Sunni Muslims, the caliph was the last in a line of spiritual and temporal rulers dating back to the Prophet's death in 632 AD. In an October 2001 videotape, Bin Laden pointedly referred to the 'humiliation and disgrace' that Islam had suffered for 'more than 80 years'. The caliphate lasted some 1400 years, the apex of Islamic identity, before it was destroyed by a potent mix of modernist ideas delivered by Western imperialism. Osama bin Laden clearly felt he had grievance on his side. Two questions flow from this, however: is there any grand plan, let alone strategy, for the restoration of the caliphate? And does the notion have any support in the wider Sunni Muslim world? On both counts, there is little that should give Osama bin Laden, his supporters, or his successors any heart. Their violence against both non-Muslims and 'un-Muslims' is set against a fanciful backdrop.

In July 2005, Ayman al-Zawahiri wrote a long letter to Abu Musab al-Zarqawi, by then head of al-Qaeda in Iraq (killed in an American air strike in June 2006).

The letter was seized during an American counter-terrorism operation and posted on the Internet by the Bush administration. In it, al-Zawahiri argued that the 'victory of Islam' required a Muslim state to be established 'in the manner of the Prophet in the heart of the Islamic world, specifically in the Levant [the area loosely covering Israel and the Palestinian areas, Jordan, Lebanon and Syria], Egypt, and the neighbouring states of the Peninsula [Saudi Arabia and the Gulf states] and Iraq'. Zawahiri set out a four-stage plan: expulsion of the Americans from Iraq; developing Islamic authority over Sunni areas in Iraq until it achieved 'the level of a caliphate'; extending 'the jihad wave' to the secular states neighbouring Iraq; and, finally, a showdown with Israel, which had been established 'only to challenge any new Islamic entity'.

In mid-2005, the Jordanian journalist Fouad Hussein published *Al-Zarqawi: the second generation of al-Qaeda*. Based on Hussein's correspondence with al-Qaeda members, this Arabic-language book set out the movement's seven-stage path to the restoration of the caliphate as follows:

- THE AWAKENING, covering the period from 9/11 to the fall of Baghdad to US forces in March 2003, with 9/11 aimed at provoking the US into declaring war on the Islamic world and thereby 'awakening Muslims'. Hussein wrote that the first phase was judged by al-Qaeda strategists as very successful: 'The battle field was opened up and the Americans and their allies became a closer and easier target.'

- OPENING EYES, lasting until 2006, during which Iraq would become the centre for al-Qaeda's global operations, with an 'army' set up there, and bases established in other Arabic states.

- ARISING AND STANDING UP, lasting from 2007 to 2010. The focus would be on Syria, with attacks on Turkey and Israel. Hussein concluded that countries neighbouring Iraq, such as Jordan, would also be in danger.

- COLLAPSE OF ARAB GOVERNMENTS, between 2010 and 2013. al-Qaeda aimed to bring about the collapse of Arab regimes and a steady growth in its own power. Oil suppliers would also be attacked and the US economy targeted through 'cyber terrorism'.

- DECLARATION OF THE CAPLIHATE, between 2013 and 2016. Western influence in the Islamic world would be so reduced and Israel so weakened that resistance was not feared. al-Qaeda hoped that the 'Islamic state' would bring about a new world order.

- TOTAL CONFRONTATION: with the declaration of the caliphate, the 'Islamic army' would pursue the fight between 'believers and non-believers'.

• FINAL VICTORY, with the rest of the world so beaten down by 1.5 billion Muslims that the success of the caliphate would be assured by 2020, at the latest.

To non-Muslims and most Muslims alike, the 'strategy' probably reads like a plot for a Dan Brown novel devised by a committee. Still, Lawrence Wright wrote in *The New Yorker* in September 2006 that it was chilling to read Hussein's book 'and realise how closely recent events seem to be hewing to al-Qaeda's forecasts'. We might note here that, no matter how it is presented publicly, the US inevitably will retreat from Iraq, leaving a mess behind and inviting a 'vindication' of al-Qaeda's strategy. Bin Laden and his followers have often cited US retreats from Vietnam, from Lebanon and, most importantly in their eyes, from Somalia, as history marching in their favour. In May 1998, bin Laden told American journalist John Miller, 'We have seen in the last decade the decline of the American government and the weakness of the American soldier'—ready to wage cold wars, but unprepared to fight long ones.

Yet it would seem most unwise for al-Qaeda to rely on support for the caliphate from Middle Eastern Muslims. Another University of Maryland/Zogby International survey, conducted in October 2005, suggested that, while a sizeable minority (36 per cent) sympathised with al-Qaeda's confrontation with America, only 7 per cent supported its methods of operation. Worse still, for al-Qaeda, only 6 per cent sympathised with its goal of creating an Islamic state. Those figures have not changed since 2005. Bin Laden's biographer, Peter Bergen, wrote early in 2007 that, for bin Laden, the restoration of the caliphate meant 'installation of Taliban-style theocracies stretching from Indonesia to Morocco'. Bergen noted, though, that a 2003 poll conducted in Saudi Arabia, 'perhaps the world's most conservative Muslim country', showed that, while 49 per cent of Saudis admired bin Laden, only 5 per cent 'wanted to live in a bin Laden state'. Bin Laden's opposition to Western ways, though not to Western technology, appeals to many Muslims. But such admiration clearly has its limits.

The Sunni–Shia divide also poses a quandary for proponents of a restored Sunni caliphate, particularly one in which Shia-majority Iraq is a central element. Al Zarqawi was no friend of the Shia, describing them in early 2004 as 'the insurmountable obstacle, the lurking snake, the crafty and malicious scorpion, the spying enemy more cunning than their Crusader masters'. Ayman al Zawahiri shared al Zarqawi's distaste for the Shia, arguing that 'any rational person' understood their connivance in the US invasion of Afghanistan, and the later overthrow of Saddam Hussein and the occupation of Iraq, whiuch led to the Shia's assumption of power. Yet, alive to the public relations dimension of al-Qaeda activities, al-Zawahiri warned al-Zarqawi—whose reputation for egregious violence was second to none—that many of the Muslim 'common folk' questioned his attacks on the Shia, especially on mosques and Shia shrines. 'We are in a battle,' al-Zawahiri wrote, 'more than half of which was taking place in the battlefield of the media … a race for the hearts and minds of our umma [community].'

Certainly, many Muslims outside the Middle East, as well as those within, appear less than impressed with al-Qaeda's goals and methods. They fear both for their religion and their own identity. Some leading non-Arab Muslims view extremist Islamism with disdain, and 'Arabism' with reservation. These doubts were conveyed tellingly in *Voices of Islam in Southeast Asia: a contemporary sourcebook*, a ground-breaking study by two Australian academics, Virginia Hooker and Greg Fealy. Noting the various influences shaping south-east Asian Islam, they wrote that, at the syncretic end of the spectrum, many Muslims regarded the blending of Islamic and pre-existing religious practices not only as permissible, but desirable. The resulting 'localised' Islam had greater spiritual and cultural richness for the region's Muslims, who saw 'Arabisation' as incompatible with and dangerous to their social traditions and dynamics. At the other end of the spectrum were those who sought the strict application of Middle Eastern norms and rituals, and who argued that 'indigenous' Islam was tainted. Hooker and Fealy quoted Abdurrahman Wahid, one-time leader of Indonesia's largest Islamic organisation, the conservative Nahdatul Ulama, and later the country's president, as warning of the dangers 'of Arabisation ... of identifying oneself with Middle Eastern cultures'. Not only did this take 'us away from our own cultural roots', but it may not be 'appropriate for our needs'.

The track record of Islamists in power—for example, in Iran, Afghanistan, and Sudan—is hardly a ringing endorsement of the claim that 'Islam is the answer'. Certainly, the importance of the Iranian revolution in overthrowing a secularist regime and installing a fundamentalist Muslim one, and sending shock waves through both the non-Muslim and Muslim worlds, should never be underestimated. The Iranian revolution, like other great upheavals, may have devoured many of its children. But it is not yet spent. Iran's challenge to the Arab world involves national pride, imperial dreams, and theological outreach. It will prove a potent mix.

Understanding the dynamics of Islam's internal contest is not just a challenge for Muslims. There is a challenge, too, for the non-Muslim worlds, especially those of Judaism and Christianity. Do they have the intellectual fortitude to draw the same distinctions about the Muslim world they draw about their own: that those within Judaism who advocate the ethnic cleansing of Palestinians from the 'Land of Israel' speak for themselves, and not for Jews more broadly; that the Klu Klux Klan and others preaching violent racism in Christ's name represented a disfigurement, not an embodiment of Christian belief; and that the fact that succession to the British monarchy formally excludes Roman Catholics reflects an historical anachronism, not modern-day religious bigotry.

What is disappointing is the chronic tendency for Islamic extremists to blame the West and other external forces for all of Islam's ills, and the tendency for Islam's critics to hold it solely responsible for its problems. The West contributed to Islam's decline; that much is history. Only those within the faith can restore it—if they want to. They will not save their religion by condemning it to being a prisoner of the past. al-Qaeda and extremist Islamism more broadly have painted Muslims into a corner, inflicting grave damage on the image of Islam, not merely in the West and the broader international community—where Muslim, Islamist, and terrorist are often used falsely, as though the terms are interchangeable—but within the Muslim world itself.

Shortly after 9/11, the former deputy prime minister of Malaysia Anwar Ibrahim, then in jail on politically inspired sodomy and corruption charges, wrote that never in Islam's history had 'the actions of so few of its followers caused the religion and its community of believers to be such an abomination in the eyes of others'. How, in the 21st century, Ibrahim wondered, could the Muslim world 'have produced an Osama bin Laden?' His answer was hardly original, but reflected an important non-Arab Muslim view of the diseased state of the political and social order of the Arab world.

There, the numbers of educated and young professionals increased year after year—people who needed space to express their political and social concerns. But with state control total, there was 'no room for civil society to grow', no genuine promotion of democracy and openness. Moreover, the ruling autocrats in Muslim countries used 'their participation in the global war against terrorism to terrorise their critics and dissenters'. Intellectuals and politicians had to find the courage to condemn fanaticism in all its forms. They had also to 'condemn the tyrants and oppressive regimes that dash every hope of peaceful change'.

How much should Islam be held to account for the conspicuous inadequacies of the Arab Middle East—the failures of modernisation, of political plurality and gender equality, of economic development and diversification and the development of social and economic safety nets, of the provision of adequate educational opportunities and health care? Are Islam's former glories (felt most keenly in the Arab world) a burden on the future progress of its followers? Anwar Ibrahim wrote that those with the clearest sense of past Muslim grandeur are at risk of being imprisoned by it, of failing to come to terms with present-day realities. The 'less illustrious history' of south-east Asian Muslims, he argued, might explain their greater capacity to come to terms with modernity: 'The Arabs, Turks or Persians are weighed down by the millstones of greatness ... the

Malays are less haunted by the ghosts of the past, more attentive to present realities, and have a greater awareness of their many shades and nuances.'

Any serious reformation of Islam must start with education—both in terms of who gets educated, where, and how. A telling pointer to the challenge is the fact that, in the early years of the 21st century, only around half of eligible secondary students in Saudi Arabia were enrolled outside the religious sector (compared, for example, to 81 per cent in Egypt). The proportions in Saudi higher education were even worse, with two of every three doctorates involving Islamic studies. Young Saudis, Robert Baer wrote in *Atlantic* magazine, were being educated 'to take part in a world that will exist only if the Wahhabi jihadists succeed in turning back the clock not just a few decades but a few centuries.' True, this is not merely a problem of Saudi or Arab Islam. British writer and historian William Dalrymple's fascinating account of Muslim education in Pakistan, *Inside the Madrasas*, argued that there were as many as 800,000 students in this entirely free Islamic education system, which ran parallel to the moribund state sector. An estimated 15 per cent of the madrasas preached violent jihad, while a few were said 'to provide covert military training'. While madrasas might be more dominant in Pakistan's educational system, Dalrymple argued that the general trend was 'common throughout the Islamic world'.

In Egypt, despite the high percentage of students in the state sector, the number of teaching institutes 'dependent on the Islamic university of al-Azhar increased from 1,855 in 1986 to 4,314 ten years later.' Egypt, the only Arab country to have produced a Nobel Prize-winning author, has a depressingly poor adult literacy rate, both male and female. According to the fourth AHD report, male literacy rates across the Arab world ranged from a low of 63 per cent in Morocco to an impressive 95 per cent in Jordan, which was only outdone by the Palestinian Territories, at 96 per cent. Egypt had the second-worst result, 67 per cent, followed by Sudan, at 69 per cent. Female literacy rates followed a similar pattern, ranging from a low of 29 per cent in Yemen to 85 per cent in Jordan and 87 per cent in the Palestinian Territories. Two countries occasionally cited as making cautious moves towards reform and democratisation—Egypt and Morocco—had less-than-flattering female literacy rates of 44 per cent and 38 per cent respectively. Even strife-torn Sudan did better, at 50 per cent.

Education, and the social and economic liberation that it can (but does not necessarily) bring, must be a critical component of any change for the better. But it appears to offer double-edged benefits. It can increase support for the peaceful resolution of conflicts. Yet, as evidenced by al-Qaeda, many young Muslim men attracted to extremism are from middle-class, well-educated backgrounds. The question here is *where* they were educated, as well as how much. Those away from family and friends become susceptible to extremist influences, perhaps in the form of a charismatic 'father' figure. We delude ourselves if we think that educational reform can fix the problems of Islam in the Arab world without political reform of the latter. Indeed, it may simply produce more young men, especially, who combine an understanding of the modern world with an inability to participate productively in it — in other words, technologically savvy fodder for al-Qaedism.

Clausewitz's famous dictum that politics was war by other means can be reworked to fit the Arab world. There, religion is politics by other means. This is not merely because of Islam's holistic view of the world; it results from the fact that the mosque has long offered a degree of cover for political activities generally not possible in the legislature or on the street. Until Middle Eastern political leaders allow greater popular participation, there is little incentive for those in the mosque to allow a dividing line to be drawn between their activities and those in the secular world beyond. To this blurring of spiritual and temporal activities, we should add the blurring of religion and nationalism in the Israeli–Palestinian conflict.

It is all too easy for Israel and its partisan supporters to point the finger at Hamas' evil intentions towards the Jewish state, in the process conveniently overlooking two factors. One is Israel's own earlier role in supporting Hamas as a counterweight to the Palestinian Liberation Organisation. The second is the contest within Hamas between pragmatists (a better term than 'moderates' to describe those prepared to accept the reality of Israel's existence) and hardliners, wedded implacably to the destruction of the Jewish state. For more than a decade, Hamas, conscious of the strong current of nationalism within Palestinian politics and society, worked to project an image that married a distinctly nationalist identity with a broader Islamic one. As the prospects of nationhood diminished — not all Hamas' doing, by any means — the religious aspects, including links with Shia Iran and Hizballah, became increasingly evident. An Israeli–Palestinian conflict defined in starkly religious terms will owe much to Israeli and US policy, as well as to Islam's own world-view. Even the seemingly 'modernist' Palestinian president Mahmud Abbas cast the conflict in such terms. In March 2007, he described an Arab League proposal as Israel's last chance for peace with the Muslim world, an opportunity for Israel to 'live in a sea of peace that begins in Nouakchott [the capital of Islamic Mauritania in West Africa] and ends in Indonesia [with the world's largest Muslim population]'.

While keen to burnish their Islamic credentials, Middle Eastern autocrats will continue to use fear of Islamist extremism to blunt both domestic and foreign criticism of their rule. By threatening Middle Eastern autocrats, extremist Islamism helped them justify their autocracy. For both rulers and ruled, religion remains a weapon in the political armoury.

The contest in the Middle East between those who want to place Islam at the core of everyday thought and activity, and those who acknowledge its appeal and influence but wish to corral it, will sharpen in the coming decades. The explanations for this are complex, but result from the deep sense of malaise within the Arab world, the continuing Israeli–Palestinian conflict — which provides both excuse and justification — and misguided US policies, which have confused, angered, and empowered the 'wrong' people. In *Dying to Win*, Robert Pape wrote that, post-9/11, the US has embarked 'on a policy to conquer Muslim countries … to remake Muslim societies in the Persian Gulf'. In a masterly understatement, he commented that 'the close association between foreign military occupations and the growth of suicide terrorist movements in the occupied regions should make us hesitate over any strategy centering on the transformation of Muslim societies by means of heavy military power'. Fouad Ajami wrote in 2003 that the American endeavour in Iraq should be driven by the task of modernising the Arab world', and that Arab objections should be dismissed as mere 'road rage'. Given his academic credentials, Ajami, if not George Bush perhaps, should have been keenly aware that 'modernisation' would risk much more than bent fenders. An Iraq in tatters; extremist Islamism on the march; American standing at an all-time low, Iran unleashed—it is hard to see any comfort in this, now or into the future. If this is road rage, God spare us a crash.

No matter how fervently the Muslim past is recollected, it cannot be undone, or changed, or relived any more in Islam than in any other faith. Today, Islam is held hostage by those who want to recreate a past that can only ever exist again in the imagination. In pursuing this goal, they have taken their religion prisoner; they have cast a profound shadow over all its adherents; and they have given a perniciously religious flavour to much international conflict. The response of the non-Muslim world to the challenge of violent Islam has often been heavy-handed and self-defeating. The gravest error has been to risk the support of hundreds of millions of ordinary Muslims who have borne and will continue to bear the brunt of extremist Islam.

It needs emphasising that only a tiny minority of the world's Islamic community is bent on violence. The findings of a Pew Global Attitudes Survey, released in mid-2007, showed strong opposition to suicide bombings across the Muslim world. In strife-torn Pakistan, a total of 81 per cent of respondents said such attacks were rarely or never justified. In Indonesia, the corresponding figure was 90 per cent. Within the Arab world, 83 per cent of Egyptians, 78 per cent of Moroccans, 76 per cent of Kuwaitis, 69 per cent of Jordanians, and 66 per cent of Lebanese fell into this category. Respondents in the Palestinian territories stood out as supporters of suicide bombing, with a total of 70 per cent stating that it was often or sometimes justified. The corresponding total for Lebanon was 34 per cent, 23 per cent for Jordan, and 21 per cent in Kuwait.

However concerned we might be about Palestinian support for suicide attacks, these figures should make it clear that the problem lies not with Islam as a whole, but with some Muslims whose own 'crusade' is directed at anyone and anything outside their narrow, dogmatic world-view. Still, a tiny minority of 1.3 billion people can and will cause a lot of headaches and heartaches for their co-religionists and the world at large.

CHAPTER FOUR

A Demographic Gulf

If there is safety in numbers, by rights the Arab world should be increasingly secure. Overall population growth rates declined in the last decades of the twentieth century, with dramatic reductions in the UAE and Saudi Arabia. But the current fertility rate (births per woman) in the Arab world remains 3.7, much higher than the average of 2.9 for all developing countries, and 1.8 for OECD states. By 2020, the Arab world will have some 430 million people, an increase of around 150 million in 20 years. Some 300 million will live in the five most populous Arab states: Egypt, Sudan, Algeria, Iraq, and Morocco.

But, far from adding to the region's security, these figures spell trouble. Simply put, the Arab world is running out food and water, and is falling far behind in creating jobs for its burgeoning workforce. The consequences will be profound, for individuals and nation states alike. Statistics can be a problem—outdated, unreliable, and eye-glazing, all at once — but they still offer a valuable snapshot of present realities and future trends. They also illustrate the marked variation between individual Arab states. A dramatic example involves life expectancy. Here, the overall trend across the Arab world is positive. By 2020, life expectancy will average 69 for men, and 71 for women — well below the OECD average and that for Israel, but respectable nonetheless. These bald figures, however, mask extraordinary regional differences. By 2020, for example, Kuwaiti men and women can expect to live 32 years longer that their Djibouti counterparts. There is also significant variation in population growth rates. While its population will be approaching 100 million by 2020, Egypt is a success story, with its population growth rate now slowed, and its maternal mortality rate halved. The UAE and Saudi Arabia, too, have cut their annual population growth rate, though Saudi Arabia's will still be near 3 per cent in 2020. But, for the region as a whole, the damage has been done. So-called 'demographic momentum' means that even relatively small growth will produce intense pressure on resources and on the regimes that control them.

For some countries, the future is nightmarish. Even though it will continue to have one of the highest infant and maternal mortality rates in the Arab world (after Somalia, Djibouti, Mauritania, and Sudan), Yemen's population will still double to 36 million by 2020, and double again by mid-century. Of greater strategic and political importance, the population of the Gaza Strip and the West Bank will grow by more than 3 per cent a year, leading to a total population of more than six million in 2020. By then, Israel's population will be approaching 10 million, with the proportion of Israeli Arabs possibly increasing from the current one-fifth to about one-third. Short of dramatic shifts, such as a major increase in Jewish migration to Israel or the 'transfer' of its Arab minority—either forcibly or through an unlikely resolution of the Arab–Israeli conflict—the Jewish State is set to become increasingly less Jewish.

Population growth raises a host of issues: health, education, employment, social services, and women's rights. The wide disparity in health services is starkly illustrated in the availability of doctors. Here, the top five, on the data compiled by the AHD reports, were Lebanon, Qatar, Egypt, Jordan, and the UAE. The worst performers were Somalia, Djibouti, Sudan, Yemen, and Morocco. Lebanon had 325 doctors for every 100,000 people; Somalia, only four. Not surprisingly, Somalia was also the worst performer for maternal mortality, with more than 1,000 deaths per 100,000 live births (against an average of 270 for the region as a whole). Somalia also topped the infant mortality rate (133 for every 1,000 live births against an Arab states average' of 48).

In 1990, five Arab states had adult literacy rates of less than 50 per cent. Just over a decade later, the number had dropped to two. In the same period, the number of states with adult literacy rates of less than 60 per cent had declined from 10 to six. Thanks largely to the United Nations Relief and Works Agency for Palestine Refugees, the Gaza Strip and the West Bank scored highest for both male and female literacy (96 and 87 per cent respectively), followed by Jordan, Kuwait, Libya, and Syria. The worst performers were Morocco (63 and 38 per cent), Egypt, Yemen, and Sudan. Wide disparities in male and female literacy abounded. The UAE was the only country in which female literacy rates outranked male (81 to 76 per cent).

Education, of course, is about quality and relevance as much as quantity. In key states such as Saudi Arabia, the focus on religious instruction educated children for the next life, not this one. Elsewhere, the heavy focus on social sciences and humanities prepared students poorly for employment in a technologically driven world. A 2007 World Bank report, *The Road Not Traveled: education reform in the Middle East and North Africa*, described the history of Middle Eastern education reform as 'a tale of ambition, accomplishment … and unfinished business'. There had been dramatic achievements, but education lagged. Illiteracy remained 'twice as high as East Asia and Latin America'. Adult literacy was still low, education systems failed to 'produce the skills needed in an increasingly competitive world', unemployment was particularly high among graduates, and the link between education, economic growth, income distribution, and poverty reduction was 'weak'.

What of opportunities for women? The world's wealthiest oil state, Saudi Arabia, still forbids women to drive, to work with men, or to appear in public with men who are not relatives. Its legal system is capable of condemning a female victim of gang rape to 200 lashes and six months' jail because she was in a car with a young man who was not a relative. (In this particular case, after an outcry, the verdict was overturned, and King Abdullah issued a pardon.) To regard these strictures as unworthy of a modern state is hardly a pointer to 'Western' cultural arrogance or insensitivity. The 2006 AHD report, *Towards the Rise of Women in the Arab World*, argued that the empowerment of women was 'a prerequisite for an Arab renaissance,' inseparably linked to the fate of the Arab world. Yet a mix of cultural, legal, social, economic, and political factors impeded 'women's equal access to education, health, job opportunities, citizenship rights and representation'.

In private life, tradition has combined with discriminatory laws to perpetuate inequality and subordination. In health, women, especially those from the least-developed countries, have suffered unacceptably high death rates. Despite a 'tremendous spread' of girls' education, women continued to lack opportunities. The Arab region had one of the highest rates of female illiteracy, and one of the lowest rates of enrolment. The region had witnessed a greater increase in women's involvement in economic activity than all other regions of the world, but it remained one of the lowest: 33 per cent for women over 15 years, a stark contrast to the world average of 56 per cent. (Male involvement was substantially greater, though, at 42 per cent—still one of the lowest rates in the world.) Women's weak involvement resulted from a culture in which employers preferred men, and there was a scarcity of jobs in general, wage discrimination, and high birth rates. Laws hindered women's freedom by requiring a father's or husband's permission for them to work, to travel, or to borrow from financial institutions. There had been progress in reducing the gender gap in education, in lowering fertility rates, and in increasing women's employment opportunities. But this was a long way off from placing them on an equal footing with men.

With its characteristic caution, the World Bank has concluded that the gender gap remains 'a challenge for the region'. Educational advances have not flowed into 'gender empowerment indicators', such as economic and political participation. The bank noted that women's share of seats in national parliaments was used to track progress toward the Millennium Development Goal of gender equality and empowerment of women. Depending on one's viewpoint, progress in the Arab world had been stunning (an almost 400 per cent increase by 2003 in the number of female national parliamentarians), or pathetic (a grand total of 11 women across the Middle East that year). It is not just a matter of raw numbers. The AHD report observed that, with the exception of the Gulf states, women had acquired the right to vote and to be candidates in parliamentary elections in the 1950s and 1960s. The number of Arab countries with women ministers had increased 'to the extent that women now participate in all governments except that of Saudi Arabia'. But this involvement was more for show than substance, with those women in power 'often selected from the ranks of the elite or appointed from the ruling party as window dressing for the ruling regimes'. Of the 15 Arab countries surveyed, an average of 6.4 per cent parliamentary seats were held by women. The figures ranged from 23 per cent in Tunisia, and 12 per cent in Syria, to 0 per cent in the UAE, Kuwait, and Saudi Arabia.

Family laws place females in a subordinate position to men. With these laws often drawn from traditional interpretations of Islamic law, women and girls need guardians—fathers, husbands, or other male relatives. Yet women activists have had some success in arguing for Islam's egalitarian nature. In Morocco, reform of the family code removed the obligation for a wife to obey her husband, allowed a wife to include a condition in the marriage contract requiring that her husband refrain from taking other wives, and established divorce as a prerogative of both men and women. Elsewhere, traditional male-centric practices remain strongly entrenched. The Algerian constitution, for example, enshrined equal rights for men and women. But, while women have had the right to file for divorce since 2005, they still cannot marry without written male permission, and are still classed as minors by Algerian family law.

A variety of commentators have warned of the 'bow wave' of youth set to engulf the Middle East. Anthony Cordesman has described the region as a long-term 'demographic nightmare', with population growth creating a 'youth explosion'. This is certainly true in absolute numbers. A 2005 report prepared by the United Nations Economic and Social Commission for West Asia projected that, between 2000 and 2020, the population aged 0–14 would increase by 29 million to 138 million, with the 15–24 age segment growing by 30 million to 78 million. By 2020, the 0–24 group, some 216 million, will make up 50 per cent of the total population across the Arab world. The impact of the youth bulge will vary significantly from state to state, but the absolute numbers are frightening. They are compounded by the fact that, by 2020, demographic hotspots such as Yemen will have a 0–24 age segment of 66 per cent. In the Palestinian territories, 60 per cent of the population will be aged 24 or less. Demographic experts note the 'bonus' that can occur when a large, young, healthy, and well-trained population is absorbed productively into the national economy. Yet, for most Arab states, antiquated education sectors and congested workplaces will remain the norm. They will be swamped by the youth bow-wave.

Employment data is notoriously rubbery, but the trends are clear. Only 47 per cent of the Arab world's working-age population is employed—the lowest rate in the world. With the demographic bulge now coming of age, young people, in the World Bank's quaint phraseology, are 'underrepresented among the region's employed'. The bank projects that nearly 40 million people will join the labour force in the decade to 2010, 'an astounding 40 per cent increase'. For the Arab world to reach the current European Union employment rate of 64 per cent by 2020, another 79 million jobs will have to be created. To reach the EU's ambitious goal of an employment rate of 70 per cent, nearly 100 new million jobs will be required.

The prospect of making any meaningful headway in meeting these needs is remote. In 2007, the World Bank concluded that many of the region's development challenges were still attributable 'to significant deficiencies in governance'. These ranged from a lack of public-sector efficiency, accountability, and honesty to the lack of transparency and contestability in government decision-making. On corruption, the AHD report observed that in some Arab states, 'both law and custom decree that the land and its natural resources belong to the ruler … private property of the ordinary citizen becomes a grant from the ruler'. In such a situation, it was difficult to talk of corruption. Whatever the ruler did or did not do with 'state' assets, he was merely 'disposing of his own property'.

The United Nations has projected unemployment rates in 2020 from 1 to 2 per cent in the oil-rich Gulf states to around 29 per cent in Algeria. A 2004 poll conducted in Saudi Arabia put unemployment ahead of religious extremism or women's rights as an issue of concern. (Estimates of the Saudi unemployment rate vary widely, muddied by the reality that many working-age Saudis, including 90 per cent of women, do not actively seek work.) Compounding the broader problem is the unemployment rate for those under 24: between 40 to 50 per cent in Algeria both for men and women; as high as 50 per cent for women in Jordan; 25 per cent for men and 39 per cent for women in Saudi Arabia; and 21 per cent and 40 per cent in Egypt. Unemployment complicates the 'marriage revolution' taking place across the Arab world—with women marrying later, and to men closer to their own age. A 'no job, no wedding' reality has unwelcome social (and, possibly, political) implications much wider than frustrated would-be happy couples.

The Gaza Strip, with unemployment possibly as high as 50 per cent amid grinding poverty, will remain a classic example of the potentially explosive link between economic, social, political, and strategic factors. In early 2008, Jordan's Queen Rania wrote that Palestinians were once reputed to be among the best-educated people in the Middle East. The UN, often maligned by Israel and its one-eyed supporters, could take much credit for this. Yet, Queen Rania continued, years of violence, isolation, and poverty had shattered this proud tradition of educational excellence. The January 2008 semester exams at UN-operated schools in Gaza 'found 50–60 per cent failure rates in mathematics and a 40 per cent failure rate in Arabic — the children's native language'. Let the world take note, the Queen demanded, 'that conditions are worse today than at any time since the occupation began'. Seventy-nine per cent of Gazan households lived in poverty; eight out of ten depended on food assistance; nearly half the labour force was unemployed; local industry had collapsed; and water and sewage systems were failing. The prospect of hundreds of thousands of young Gazan men with time on their hands and nothing to do other than absorb the messages of their increasingly hardline political leaders should send a chill through Israeli spines — and anyone who still entertains the notion of a peaceful resolution of the Israeli–Palestinian conflict.

New entrants into the Arab workforce are arriving with higher education levels, a potentially important shift in an era of would-be 'knowledge-based' economies. Yet higher education is no guarantee of employment. This is especially true for Arab women. Even those with similar levels of education to men have unemployment rates two to three times higher. Part of the explanation is the broad decline in the public sector—historically, the employer of first resort for Arab women, whose preference for studying the humanities undermines their employment prospects in the business world.

Across the Arab world, agriculture has long provided both a way of employing people and disguising unemployment. It will continue to employ one-quarter to one-third of the workforce in Egypt, Syria, Tunisia, Algeria, Morocco, and Oman; as much as half the workforce in Yemen; and around 60 per cent in Sudan. Yet the agriculture sector is in decline in all Arab states, undermining a traditional economic and social safety net, increasing dependency on imported foods, and fuelling urbanisation and 'hyper-urbanisation'. In the past quarter-century, the number of city dwellers across the Arab world has more than doubled, to some 200 million people. Egypt's urban population, at 43 per cent of the total, is low by regional standards. (Kuwait leads with 98 per cent, followed by Lebanon, Jordan, Libya, and Saudi Arabia). Still, Cairo's population doubled to around 12 million people.

Whether in cities or the countryside, one non-negotiable commodity is water. Arab governments and people face a dismal future as occupants of the most water-scarce region in the world. Most Arab states already fall below the international threshold of 1,000 cubic metres of freshwater per person per year. With 5 per cent of the world's total population, the Arab world has around 1 per cent of the world's annual renewable water resources. Conceivably, in 20 years' time the ratios might still be the same—but another 150 million people will be competing for those same scarce water supplies. Population pressure is exhausting natural water supplies, with demand for water exceeding supply in nearly half the countries in the region. Annual renewable water supplies have been halved since 1960. They will be halved again over the next 20 years. The World Bank estimates that the water available per person could fall by as much as 50 per cent by 2050.

Water sources vary from country to country. Egypt and Iraq rely mostly on surface water from large international rivers. Egypt's very existence relies on the waters of the Nile, a dependency that can only grow as the country's population nears the 100 million mark. An ambitious Egyptian plan to spend an estimated $70 billion over the next 10 years to reclaim nearly 1.4 million hectares of desert has drawn fire from conservationists, who question the logic of using precious water resources to grow food in such a hostile environment. The plan also has implications for Egypt's relations with other Nile basin countries, especially Sudan and Ethiopia, who have long been unhappy with Egypt's consumption of more than half the Nile's water. Yemen and the Gulf states depend almost entirely on groundwater or, in the case of the Gulf oil states who can afford it, on desalinisation. Water is also a critical element in the Israeli–Palestinian conflict. Elsewhere, non-Arab Turkey's 'superior' upstream location as the headwaters both of the Tigris and the Euphrates rivers has helped it to dictate water policy to downstream states such Syria and Iraq, both of whom are critically dependent on river water for irrigation. Turkey has also used water as a weapon to pressure Syria with over the Kurdish issue.

Across the region, the human impact on precious water resources is all too evident. The Gulf countries have the highest per-capita consumption of domestic water in the world—some 50 per cent per person more than in the US, which is hardly a model of restraint itself. Over-pumping of 'fossil' ground water is reducing aquifers in Morocco's agriculturally vital Oum Er Rbia River basin by some five metres a year. Yemen's Ministry of Water and the Environment has described the country as the most water-constrained in the world; in some areas, the water table is falling by up to eight metres annually. Over-pumping of the West Bank aquifer, and the generous allocations to Israeli settlers over the needs of the local Palestinian population, adds another layer of sharpness to the already bitter Israeli–Palestinian relationship.

Middle Eastern states and peoples, of course, are well used to managing severe heat and water shortages. This is just as well, because their problems of too little water and too many people will only increase, further complicated by climate change. As one of the world's most water-scarce regions, highly reliant on agriculture, and with a large share of its population and economic activity in flood-prone coastal zones, climate change is more bad news for the Arab world. The International Panel on Climate Change (IPCC) estimates that the Middle East will become even hotter and drier, and therefore more drought-prone. By 2025, an additional 80–100 million people will be exposed to 'water stress'. This is likely to result in an even greater pressure on groundwater resources, which the IPCC says are already 'being extracted in most areas beyond the aquifers' recharge potential'. Temperature increases could expose as many as 25 million people to coastal flooding. Heat waves, water scarcity, and decreasing water and air quality 'are likely to affect public health, and more generally lead to challenging living conditions'. With global models predicting sea levels rising by up to 0.3 metres by 2050, and 0.9 meters by 2100, low-lying coastal areas in Tunisia, Qatar, Libya, the UAE, Kuwait, and Egypt in particular will be at great risk.

Climate change poses great challenges to the region's cities, which are hubs for its economic, social, cultural, and political activity. Rising sea levels could affect 43 port cities in the Middle East and in North Africa. A sea-level rise of half a metre would leave more than two million people displaced in the Egyptian coastal city of Alexandria, threatening to devastate this important financial and historical centre. Egyptian environmental experts have warned that, from around 2020, some 15 per cent of the agriculturally crucial Nile delta could be threatened by rising sea levels and the seepage of saltwater into groundwater supplies. Climate change could also produce more severe sandstorms, longer droughts, worse floods, and increased evaporation of the vital waters of the Nile.

Climate change will inflict another, paradoxical, cost on Middle Eastern food importers — including Egypt, one of the world's largest consumers of foreign wheat. Pressure in the US, Europe, and elsewhere to use increasing quantities of grain for bio-fuel production will mean less food for export, higher prices, the prospect of growing food shortages, and the possibility of worsening food riots. The World Bank has blamed a dramatic increase in world food prices in recent years on the increased use of crops for bio-fuels rather than food. Within the next decade, according to the United Nations Food and Agriculture Organisation, the US will double the amount of corn it diverts to bio-fuel, and European use of wheat for bio-fuel will increase twelve-fold. High oil prices play a mostly pernicious role in the picture (apart from delivering huge windfalls to Middle Eastern oil exporters). By encouraging energy diversification, they push more foods into bio-fuel production. This might stimulate agricultural production, but higher oil prices mean higher agricultural costs through, for example, increased shipping and fertiliser costs. Those literally at the bottom of the food chain, and not just in the Middle East, face an increasingly problematic future. In a dramatic illustration of the food versus fuel dilemma, in late 2007 the UN Special Rapporteur on the Right to Food, Jean Ziegler, denounced biofuels as a 'crime against humanity'.

Faced with an uncertain future in an increasingly crowded and arid landscape, it is little wonder that many young Arabs seek to escape. Over 50 per cent of young men surveyed by for the AHD report defined their 'career plan' as immigration. Of these, a majority looked to Europe, and just over one-third to the US or Canada. This is not necessarily welcomed by the would-be host countries. The former vice-chairman of the CIA's National Intelligence Council, Herbert Meyer, wrote caustically in 2007 that most countries in the Western world had stopped breeding, a remarkable development for a civilisation 'obsessed with sex'. With the prospect of there being 70 to 80 million fewer Europeans in 30 year's time than there are today, and a decline of 30 per cent in the working-age population, 'European countries are currently importing Moslems'. In Meyer's view, the failure to integrate these new arrivals into the cultures of their host countries amounted to 'a political catastrophe'.

Young or not-so-young Arabs who arrive in Europe, the US, or elsewhere can make a substantial contribution to their home countries through the remittances they send home, totalling billions of dollars each year. Europe has become a critical source of worker remittances. For Jordan, Yemen, Morocco, Tunisia, and Egypt, these remittances are greater as a percentage of national gross domestic product than that made by workers from India and Mexico — two major sources of international labour. But there is a curious dichotomy here. Each year, tens of billions of dollars are sent home by Indian, Pakistani, Bangladeshi, and Filipino workers living in the Gulf states. At the same time, about 25 per cent of Saudi men under the age of 25, around 20 per cent of Egyptians, and as many as 40 per cent of young Algerian men remain unemployed.

The Gulf Arab states have long provided valuable opportunities for workers from other Arab states — Egyptian, Yemenis, Sudanese, Jordanians, and Palestinians, in particular — meaning vital foreign exchange for their home countries. But their place remains much less secure than that of non-Arabs. Some 80 per cent of the UAE's population of 2.6 million are foreigners. The corresponding figure for Qatar is 56 per cent; for Kuwait, 53 per cent; and 21 per cent for Saudi Arabia. Yet a mix of economic, social, and political factors means that Arab workers have long been outnumbered, by about two to one, by labourers from the sub-continent and elsewhere in Asia. In an environment where workers are vulnerable to exploitation and maltreatment, Asian workers are regarded simply as cheaper and more manageable. They have the added advantage of mostly leaving their families at home, unlike many Arab workers who clearly view themselves as migrants and not merely contract labour.

Politics has also played a part. As many as 1.5 million Arab workers—Yemenis, Jordanians, Palestinians, and Egyptians—were expelled during the first Gulf War in 1990–91 for their actual or perceived support of Saddam Hussein. Ironically, the linguistic and cultural affinity of Arab workers has made them more politically suspect than workers from the Philippines or India. In Saudi Arabia, foreigners still make up around two-thirds of the workforce, and the government has enacted a law requiring 75 per cent 'Saudiisation'. But the focus on religious instruction and rote learning in Saudi education means that local schools are not producing readily employable people. And Saudis, not just those with connections to the royal family, have become accustomed to being subsidised not to work. As long as oil revenues remain high, Saudis remain averse to taking orders or performing work that they see as demeaning, and imported labour remains around one-third cheaper than Saudi manpower, little will change.

Can economic growth 'save' the region? Falling population growth rates and an oil-price boom sound like good news. But, oil or no oil, the Arab world is a serious underperformer. The first AHD report lamented that in 1999 the combined gross domestic product of the Arab countries totalled $531.2 billion—less than that of a single European country, Spain, whose GDP for that year reached $595.5 billion. Some commentators argued that the GDP disparity should not be exaggerated. Using 'parity purchasing power', for example, the CIA *World Factbook* put the total 2004 GDP for Arab countries at more that $1515 billion, well ahead of Spain's $938 billion. But GDP per head of population paints a gloomy picture. The best example is Saudi Arabia, which, despite its extraordinary oil wealth, has seen per-capita income collapse by nearly 75 per cent in the space of a generation.

The 2007 World Bank report, *Economic Developments and Prospects*, noted that the region was undergoing a 'remarkable period of high economic growth'. But productivity growth remained low, and labour-force participation was 'the lowest of any developing region'. The dilemma faced was that of job quality versus job quantity. Demographic pressures would push for quantity, but job quality was needed to survive a fall in oil prices. The report commented that the region's labour markets were 'at the extreme of developing countries', with the highest labour-force growth, the lowest level of female participation (ranging in 2005 from a low of 11 per cent in the Gaza Strip and the West Bank to a high of 55 per cent in Djibouti, for a region-wide average of 31 per cent), and the world's youngest labour force, except for sub-Saharan Africa. The job-creation challenge would remain greater than any other region apart from the sub-Sahara. By 2020, labour-force participation would be the lowest of any developing region. Migration provided an important mechanism for 'risk diversification', but was unlikely to contribute 'in a major way' to lowering unemployment. The task was to maintain the exceptionally high rates of employment growth in recent years, and 'provoke even greater job creation, particularly by the private sector'.

Ironically, the higher the international oil price, the less incentive for Arab oil states to pursue political or economic reform. The resource-rich labour-importing economies in the Gulf (Oman, Qatar, Saudi Arabia, and the UAE) had, in the World Bank's view, 'taken significant steps towards greater inclusiveness and accountability in government'. But labour-abundant oil economies, such as Algeria, Libya, and Syria, generally had not 'moved forward'. For all Arab states, the question remained whether reform involved mere flirtation with domestic and foreign suitors, rather than serious commitment.

The often-gloomy view of the Arab world presented in the Arab Human Development reports prompted one American academic, James Rauch, professor of economics at the University of California, to argue the meaninglessness of talking about the Arab world as an 'economic aggregate'. He divided the Arab world into three economic categories:

- Sub-Saharan: Mauritania, Sudan, Djibouti, and Yemen (the latter was included in this group because of latitude and geographic proximity);
- Oil exporting: Algeria, Libya, Saudi Arabia, Kuwait, Bahrain, Qatar, the UAE, and Oman; and
- Mediterranean: Morocco, Tunisia, Egypt, Jordan, Lebanon, and Syria.

Rauch contrasted differences in human-development indicators across the Arab world with those across Latin American countries. Life expectancy varied by 30 years across the Arab world, against 15 in Latin America; adult literacy by 49 per cent compared to 31 per cent; school enrolments by 68 per cent as against 41 per cent. Per-capita GDP across the Arab world varied by nearly $20,000 compared to a $9,000 gap across Latin American countries. The Arab world, Rauch concluded, was not a meaningful economic aggregate. He questioned the sense of putting together countries as diverse in economic circumstance and achievement as Egypt and Bahrain, or Sudan and the UAE. Still, the Arab world does project itself as a distinct cultural and linguistic grouping. Examining its joint economic record may flatter some countries and disadvantage others, but that applies to all geographic groupings. It is not unreasonable to examine the joint record of, and the challenges before, Arab states.

On education, Rauch noted comments in the first

AHD report that educational achievement in the Arab countries as a whole, judged even by traditional criteria, was still modest. He pointed out that the average period of education in 1999 was 5.7 years, an 'enormous' improvement over the 1960 figure of 1.0 year. That may be true. But the Arab world is in a global competition and is falling well behind other developing regions. The region as a whole is a serious under-achiever on many of the social and economic criteria that help to define states as modern, and the majority of them will face serious problems meeting the demands placed upon them by rapid population growth.

Looking at the Middle East in 2020, the US National Intelligence Committee commented that youth bulges would likely persist, with unemployment and underemployment among young adults, spelling 'discontent in the age cohort most susceptible to political radicalisation'. It added that a few states would make at least partially effective efforts to control population growth, but the leadership needed for such efforts would likely 'be too spotty for effective population control to be a region-wide trend'.

In 2007, the World Bank divided the Arab states into three categories:

- Resource-poor, labour-abundant economies: Egypt, Jordan, Morocco, Tunisia, Lebanon, Djibouti, Gaza and the West Bank;

- Resource-rich, labour-abundant economies: Algeria, Iraq, Syria, and Yemen; and
- Resource-rich, labour-importing economies: Saudi Arabia, United Arab Emirates, Kuwait, Libya, Qatar, Oman, and Bahrain.

Clearly, development 'challenges' and future prospects depend very much on the mix of resources and population. Those with oil money have the breathing space and funds to create alternate sources of employment other than the markedly labour-'lite' petroleum sector. But diversification is not a singular blessing. The UAE, for example, stands out in reducing its reliance on the oil and gas sector. In early 2008, its economics minister, Sheikha Lubna al-Qasimi, proudly noted that 62.5 per cent of the country's gross national product no longer came from oil production. But the UAE's success in avoiding the 'oil curse' has created another form of dependency—on foreign labour. Young Emiratis are becoming 'knowledge workers'. But 80 per cent of the UAE's population consists of foreigners, on whom the country is uncomfortably reliant.

The economics of the future Middle East cannot be decoupled from the politics: population growth will demand job creation, which will demand economic growth, driven at least partly by private investment. But capital's cowardly demeanour will make it wary of problematic places afflicted by rising domestic strife or seemingly unresolvable regional issues. Only the most romantic would envisage a reduction in regional tensions involving the Israeli–Palestinian conflict, the mess and uncertainty in Iraq, or the tensions between the Arab world and Iran. These tensions will be an important influence on oil prices, substantially benefiting leaders of the oil-producing states. Such leaders could spend oil windfalls on national development, but they are more likely to spend them by seeing off threats to their authority.

Early in 2008, *The Economist* declared that it was 'not easy to be an Arab these days':

> If you are old, the place where you live is likely to have changed so much that little seems friendly and familiar. If you are young, years of rote learning in dreary state schools did not prepare you well for this new world. In your own country you have few rights. Travel abroad and they take you for a terrorist. Even your leaders don't count for much in the wider world. Some are big on money, others on bombast, but few are inspiring or visionary.

Across the Arab world, sclerotic regimes face increasingly problematic futures driven by the demands of growing populations, the complexities of the Internet age, and the unsavoury political and strategic environment created in part by them and in part by ideologically driven foreign meddlers. But when all seems dark, there is a ready excuse for all of the Arab world's woes: Israel.

CHAPTER FIVE

Excuses, Excuses ...

Originators of the third monotheistic religion,
beneficiaries religiously and culturally of the other
two, co-sharers with the West of the Greco-Roman
tradition, holders aloft of the torch of enlightenment
throughout medieval times, generous contributors to
European renaissance, the Arabic-speaking peoples have
thus taken their place among the forward-marching
democratic nations of the world and promise to make
further contributions to the progress of mankind. The
achievement of the past is the promise of the present
for the future.

This is not a vision that came to George Bush Jr. in
a moment of alcohol or religiously inspired trance. It
is the final paragraph of the fifth edition of *The Arabs*
(published 1968) by Philip Hitti, that fine Lebanese-
born scholar of the Middle East, whose long stint at

Princeton University (until the mid-1950s) played a crucial role in developing American interest in and study of the Arab world. It is a generous comment, rightly reflecting the richness of the Arab past. It reminds those in the 'West' how much they are linked to the 'East', and that 'civilisations' are never hermetically sealed from one another. A distinctly human mix of curiosity, greed, sense of adventure, and idealism drive different peoples to rub against one another—a process that both abrades and smoothes, and both enlightens and sharpens prejudice.

It is a comment that rested on hope, but has proved largely ill-judged. True, life for many people in the Arab world has improved, sometimes markedly, since Hitti wrote these words. The trends for life expectancy, health, and education have gone in the right direction, though with great variations across the region. A few in the Arab world lead lives of a degree of opulence that most people would find unimaginable. Rightly, we take notice of what those in the Arab world say and do because of the region's capacity to shape our lives in dramatic fashion and simplified imagery—lubricating it with oil and making it unsafe with terror. But it remains a region over which many of its own people despair: a region of lost or unfulfilled opportunities; of venality, corruption and repression; and with a great capacity to diminish the lives of its citizens and many others, now and into the future.

Why did Philip Hitti's generous optimism or George

Bush's later ideological obsessions for the region prove so wayward? The question is more easily posed than answered. Yet, for some, in the region and beyond, an explanation lies readily to hand—the creation of the state of Israel as a last throw of the colonial dice when the Jewish state was imposed upon the Arab world to atone for European sin. Without Israel, and freed of Ottoman and European rule, so the argument ran, Arabs could have built their lives, educated their children, and created jobs and opportunities and hope for the future. With Israel darkening the horizon, the Arab world was condemned forever to second-class status.

Six decades on, with Israel a reality and in formal peace with several Arab states, the question hangs in their air: why is the Arab region lagging the rest of the world, in modernity, opportunity, freedom, and hope for the future? There can only be one apparent answer: Israel holds the Arab world hostage. All other issues—political liberalisation, government accountability, women's rights—are secondary to the Palestinian struggle. Only when this is resolved can the contemporary and future ills of the Arab world be remedied. Only then will it be reasonable to expect Arab leaders to focus on what ails their own societies, to address their own shortcomings, and to pursue sorely needed internal reforms. Gamal Mubarak, touted as a possible successor to his father as Egypt's president—and a supposed moderniser—warned in 2004, for example, that reform had to await the end of fighting between Israelis and Palestinians. He, more than many, would have known that Israelis and Palestinians are adept at finding reasons to go on spilling each other's blood.

The very fact of Israel moulds Arab politics: it is a daily reminder of Arab failures—military, economic, educational, political, regional. Egypt's president Nasser declared after the disaster of the 1967 war that 'what is taken by force can only be retrieved by force'. His successor, Anwar Sadat, retreated from this position, recognised the Israeli state, recovered Egyptian territory—and paid the ultimate price through an assassin's bullet. Individual Arab regimes are often indifferent to the fate of Palestinians while very much alive to the cause of Palestine as a mean of diverting attention from their own shortcomings. In the brief war of 1967, Israel became the occupier of vast tracts of Arab land. The Arab states vowed no reconciliation; no recognition; no negotiation. Yet by the mid-1990s, Egypt and Jordan, key frontline states, were formally at peace with the Jewish state. Egypt defected from the Arab cause in 1978, and was expelled from Arab councils, but was eventually readmitted. What did this say about Arab unity and determination? Dealing with Israel showed up the myth of Arab unity, with the extremes ranging from full diplomatic ties (Egypt and Jordan) to trenchant opposition (Syria, supported by non-Arab, Iran). The bulk of the Arab states huddled in between, espousing the cause of peace and Palestinian statehood, knowing that they remained safe from a reality that might well turn the spotlight on their rule.

Hilal Khashan, professor of political science at the American University of Beirut, wrote in 2000 that the 'prevailing mood of despair' in the Arab world could not be explained without reference to

> the far-reaching consequences of the protracted conflict with Israel on Arab publics and ruling elites. Ambitious army officers used the Palestinian cause as a pretext for launching numerous military coups and mobilized their countries' scarce resources for the day of liberation that never came. The masses tolerated excessive human rights violations and material deprivations for the sake of reinstating the displaced Palestinians to their homeland, as well as redeeming Arab military honour. The ruling elites, having debilitated the masses by the humiliation of defeat, finally declared Israel unconquerable and resigned themselves to peace with the Jewish state which their populations interpreted as an instrument of surrender.

Arab defeats, humiliations, and back-downs made Israel a defining element in national and regional politics. In the process, they moulded Arab perceptions of the West as imposing Israel upon the Arabs for crimes committed by Europeans in Europe. For some in the

Arab world, the West added insult to injury when Saudi Arabia, Egypt, and Syria later provided military as well as political support for the American campaign to oust Saddam Hussein from Kuwait. Khashan observed that it was 'particularly agonising for the Arabs to see their leading armies show unusual vigour in fighting Iraq, none of which they had ever shown in dealing with Israel'. That is unfair to earlier Arab military actions, especially in the wars of 1948 and 1973, when Arab armed forces occasionally fought with courage and determination. But it is a question of perception as much as reality. The second Gulf war further highlighted the huge cracks in 'Arab solidarity', already revealed by the brutal eight-year war between Iraq and Persian Iran in the 1980s, during which Syria and Libya sided with Iran while the oil-producing Gulf states, as well as Egypt and Jordan, supported Iraq.

Israel showed up 'Arabism' as bombastic, hollow, and ineffectual, in the process creating a sense of victimhood on the part both of the Palestinians and the wider Arab community. In reality, any 'peace' negotiations were and remain about the final terms of Arab surrender to Israel. Yet for all the humiliation and disservice Israel brought, it also embodied the explanation for Arab failures. Right in their midst lay the explanation for Arab shortcomings, imposed upon them by a guilt-ridden West.

The argument, and the excuse, was fraudulent but potent. Israel might have much to answer for, but its existence cannot explain why women in Saudi Arabia — while now allowed to hold their own identity cards — are still forbidden to drive despite the nation's rulers' genuflections to notions of reform; why stoning is potentially still a punishment for adultery in the supposedly super-modernised UAE; why Saddam Hussein invaded Kuwait; why the Arab region's educational levels are spotty; why its labour-force participation rates are the lowest in the world; why the Arab world also sets another record low in female participation in electoral politics; and why 'honour' killings of women range in number from an estimated 20 a year in the Palestinian territories and Jordan, to 50 in Egypt, and to as many as 400 in Yemen. To hold Israel and the Israeli–Palestinian conflict accountable for the long list of the ills of the Arab world, as otherwise 'respectable' Arab leaders are prone to do, puts them, in effect, in the same belief prism as Osama bin Laden, a man they purportedly despise. To point the finger unwaveringly at the US and Israel says more about the underbelly of Arab politics than anything else.

In his *100 Myths About the Middle East*, Professor Fred Halliday observed that the Arab–Israeli conflict says nothing about the reasons for the predominance of kleptocratic family and political elites, the misuse of oil revenues, the prevalence of conservative religious censorship, the denial of the rights of workers and women, or the poor quality of education. Arab regimes, he wrote, had used the 'urgent priority' of the conflict with Israel 'as a fig leaf to deflect criticism aimed at the more repressive and undemocratic elements of their government'.

Israeli–Palestinian peace, then, could be an uncomfortable phenomenon for autocratic Arab regimes, exposing them to domestic scrutiny and criticism as never before. It might, for example, have led to public disquiet in Saudi Arabia over the new benchmark for extravagance set by Prince Alaweel bin Talal, cousin of King Abdullah and one of the world's richest individuals, when he ordered the first VIP A380 superjumbo. According to Airbus' marketing director for executive aviation, the new plane, costing around $300 million, would give the prince a lot more room, and presumably style, than his current Boeing 747 jumbo. This should be a comfort for the prince as average per-capita income in Saudi Arabia slides, and the kingdom's social and economic cracks widen. But he need not worry that peace, or public scrutiny, is in the offing. The prospect of a sustainable deal between Israelis and Palestinians, rather than occasional uneasy truces, or between Israel and the broader Arab and Iranian worlds, is a mirage.

In early 2008, Tony Blair, at his ingénue best, declared that the Arab world was 'in transition'. The question, he said, was what it would 'transition into'. The choices were either a 'cutting-edge vision' of globalisation and modernisation, or the Islamists' vision of a 'battle to the death' against the West and its allies, including Israel. The would-be modernisers, he said, regarded solving the Israeli–Palestinian conflict 'as an important part in making sure that their vision beats the other vision'. Blair commented that he spent a lot of time talking to the Arabs. Some Arab-born critics of the Arab world have observed that natural politeness, sycophancy, and fear lead many Arabs to keep their thoughts to themselves. Nonetheless, Blair's 'genuine' deduction, 'not shared by everyone in Israel', was that Arabs genuinely (that word again) 'want this settled now'. There were Arab leaders who wanted to be on the forefront of globalisation and who realised that 'their politics and their culture have got to start coming into synch with their economies'. Blair reportedly faulted Israel for tardy implementation of economic projects that could benefit both the West Bank and Gaza, and also asserted that freedom of movement for West Bank Palestinians could be improved without compromising Israeli security.

This sounds suspiciously like a gentler Israeli occupation. But whether it is gentle or harsh is now largely irrelevant. Whatever Blair's grandiose pronouncements (understandable, perhaps, as he was speaking as the newly crowned Middle East peacemaker) the two-state solution is dead. The three main suspects in for its killing are Israel, the dynamics of Palestinian politics, and a curious mix of American cowardice, inactivity, idealism, and ineptitude. Between Blair's choices of sunlit modernisation and Islamist darkness there is, in fact, a third way — skilful balancing acts by repressive regimes determined to hang on to power through playing off internal reformers, Islamists, and Western politicians. The available armoury includes appeals to Arab nationalism, heavily spiced with Islamism; de-legitimisation, harassment, and repression of critics and reformers; and the pretence of reform, including, on occasion, the granting of minor concessions to buy off internal critics and burnish international reputations.

Arab leaders will continue to espouse Israeli–Palestinian peace, knowing that there is no real danger of it happening. If it did, what might be the consequences for their self-absorbed, self-promoting rule? To add insult to injury, Israel, whatever its other shortcomings, might well provide a raucous, no-holds-barred role model for democratic practice within the Arab world. How much easier life is when flimsy democratic credentials and bombastic default settings can be sheltered by a higher purpose, 'the noble cause of Palestine'. Israel will continue to fill a very useful purpose for the Arab states as they maintain the pretence of the Arab 'nation' providing a mantle for 22 state-centric entities. Arab 'unity' was again on display in March 2008 when Saudi Arabia, Egypt, and Jordan sent junior officials to the annual Arab League summit, hosted by Syria, while Lebanon boycotted the meeting entirely. Rime Allaf, an associate fellow at Chatham House in London, wrote that, despite 'their proven futility,' the summits had always managed to create a 'modicum of expectation'. But with few exceptions, 'when actionable resolutions were adopted,' such as Egypt's expulsion in the Baghdad summit in 1979 following its peace agreement with Israel, or the emergency Cairo summit of 1990 in the aftermath of the Iraqi invasion of Kuwait, summits mostly showcased 'Arabs agreeing to disagree'. The Damascus summit followed the script faithfully.

The choices before the Arab world on Israel will not change: make peace with it, or sit tight, hoping that one day it will disappear. Not to actively make peace is, in fact, to opt for the second choice. The beauty of this is that the Arab world will not have to *do* anything. Certainly, the right noises will be made, the grand meetings convened, where peace is talked about as though it is both a desirable and realisable goal. The logic that underpins the hardline view is simple — it looks to a future without Israel. This is not necessarily today or tomorrow, next year, or even next decade, but Arab constancy will eventually triumph. This view may prove well founded, but — make no mistake — it is not driven by any special concern about the Palestinians. Israel is a mirror of Arab failure, a daily reminder that the 'Arab nation' cannot be complete as long as the Jewish state exists. These are the sentiments that Osama bin Laden has tapped. True, he, and especially al-Qaeda's tactics, may not enjoy much support throughout the Arab world. But bin Laden and time-worn Arab regimes share one important thing in common: they have little or no interest in conditioning their publics for 'normalcy' with Israel. Arab rulers perform a balancing act. This involves espousing the Palestinian cause, invoking Israel as the cause of the region's shortcomings, and yet needing Israel for their own survival.

Arabs and Israelis have long known what is required to effect a settlement. They wait for the other side to blink. What is there in the experience of the 60 years of Israel's existence that provides hope that this will change in the next 60? Leaving aside Israel's sins of omission and commission—and they are substantial—Arab leaders have trained their publics to treat Israel with deep suspicion, and then have fed off this suspicion. Even in supposedly moderate Egypt, the dangers of dealing with Israel are great. Sadat's assassination in 1981 was a dramatic example of this. But take the case of the playwright Ali Salem, expelled by the Egyptian Union of Writers in 2001 because he had visited Israel and written about it. *My Drive to Israel*, written after Salem drove to Israel in 1994, offered a sharp and whimsical view of Arab–Israeli dealings. He observed that Arab military actions against Israel had 'succeeded in relieving the Arab nation of the burden of governing a great deal of real estate' (with the Sinai, Gaza and the West Bank, and the Golan Heights falling into Israeli hands during the June 1967 war). Salem excoriated the mentality of his fellow countrymen. Talk of an Israeli cultural invasion of Egypt was 'nonsense', he wrote, born from 'a feeling of inadequacy and ignorance ... a stupid slogan chanted for demagogic purposes' that blackmailed intellectuals, and sowed fear in the young generation.

But even among Arab critics of the Arab world, there is a marked tendency to blame others for the region's shortcomings. In 2004, Samir Kassir, a prominent Lebanese journalist of Palestinian origin, produced a scathing account of the 'deep disquiet' pervading the Arab world. The picture, he wrote in *Being Arab*, was bleak from any angle. 'Apart from sub-Saharan Africa ... the Arab world is the region where men and, to an even greater extent, women, have the least chance of thriving.' The term Arab denoted 'at best, a culture that denies everything modernity stands for, suffering 'from a thoroughgoing lack of achievement'. The problem was not that of cultural predisposition, but 'the crisis of the state'. Few Arab nations were spared his pen. Even in the 'luxury emirates' of the Gulf, modernisation remained 'merely window dressing'. The same people who swore allegiance to the global economy were 'often responsible for financing that other global enterprise, jihadism'. Yet Kassir also pointed the finger at the West for its past, present, and likely future sins. While Arab victimhood portrayed Arabs as the West's primary target, 'totally disregarding the other peoples of the world, and world history in general,' the Arab world, in fact, was 'the only region on the earth where the West has continually acted as if it were the master—and still does today, either directly or through Israel'. The 'cycle of malaise' was unlikely to end soon: the persistence of the West's hegemony, exacerbated by America's occupation of Iraq and Israel's ever-growing supremacy, 'precludes a quick awakening'.

In June 2005, Kassir was murdered when his car was blown up. Not a few Arab leaders had been discomfited by the sharpness of his writings. But given that Syria had 'form' in Lebanon, given Kassir's description of Syria as combining 'the corruption of the former Soviet republics with a Chinese-style closed police state', and given that his last newspaper column, under the headline 'Mistake after mistake', attacked that Syrian Ba'ath party, the circumstantial evidence pointed unmistakably in one direction.

If Israel is the primary excuse, its principal backer, the United States, must also have much to answer for. Long before the folly of Iraq, the Arab-street view of the US was characterised by resentment of perceived American arrogance and bullying. This posed a real dilemma for states such as Egypt and Saudi Arabia and the UAE, who rely heavily on American protection and, in Egypt's case, largesse. The task before their rulers is to genuflect towards a peaceful resolution of the Israeli–Palestinian conflict for the sake of ties with the US, and at the same time ensure that their credentials as champions of the Palestinian cause keep the domestic political waters calm. They need to be especially mindful of the sentiments that shape popular thinking about the Israeli–Palestinian conflict, captured in the following extract from a poem by the Syrian poet Nizar Qabbani, written in 1998, a year before his death, and well before 9/11 fixed terrorism on the global noticeboard:

I am with Terrorism

We are accused of terrorism …

If we refuse to die

with Israel's bulldozers

tearing our land

tearing our history …

If this was our sin,

then, lo, how beautiful terrorism is?

I am with terrorism

if it is able to save me

from the immigrants from Russia

Romania, Hungary, and Poland

They settled in Palestine

set foot on our shoulders

to steal the minarets of al-Quds [Jerusalem]

and the door of Aqsa

to steal the arabesques

and the domes.

… after Olso,

we no longer had teeth:

> we are now a blind and lost people.
> I am with terrorism
> as long as this new world order
> is shared
> between Amrika and Israel
> half-half.

In the aftermath of September 11, the Saudis showed a new-found interest in resolving the Israeli–Palestinian conflict and in normalising Arab–Israeli relations. At one level, this was certainly a positive move. At another, it showed Saudi awareness of the country's image problems, especially in the US, dramatically illustrated by the fact that some three-quarters of the 9/11 hijackers were Saudi citizens. The findings of a December 2007 public opinion poll in Saudi Arabia conducted by a Washington-based group, a Terror Free Tomorrow (TFT), reflected the challenges before the Saudi leadership and its Washington supporters. Just over half of the 1000 Saudis interviewed by telephone reported a 'very' or 'somewhat' unfavourable attitude towards the United States. This was a marked improvement on a smaller poll in May 2006 that recorded an 89 per cent unfavourable view. But a worrying element in the 2007 poll for the Saudi leadership, as well as for the US and Israel, was that a slight majority of respondents viewed Iran favourably rather than unfavourably (47 versus 44 per cent). Less than 15 per cent of respondents viewed

Osama bin Laden or al-Qaeda favourably, but 36 per cent supported Saudi citizens going to Iraq to fight US forces. Respondents showed a strong antipathy towards Jews: a mere 6 per cent held favourable views; 81 per cent, 'very unfavourable' ones. Just over half said that they would oppose any peace treaty recognising Israel.

The US will continue to face a considerable policy dilemma. If the unresolved Israeli–Palestinian conflict provides cover for Arab inaction on domestic reform, the logical conclusion is to fix the conflict. But if the conflict results in part from a lack of political reform and liberalisation within the Arab world, the first goal, logically, should to 'fix' Arab politics. The latter came as an afterthought rationale for the invasion of Iraq, and lay behind Condoleezza Rice's notable debunking in Cairo in mid-2005 of six decades of American preoccupation with security over democracy (see chapter two). Unfortunately for those Arab liberals and reformers who took heart from this speech, American commitment to democracy was shown to be flimsy indeed when the US shunned the Hamas-led government delivered by the Palestinian elections in early 2006. US ideologues and Islamist extremists appear to have more in common than either would admit, both demanding the 'right' result from the electoral process.

US contrariness and back-tracking plays into the hands of Arab rulers who will select those parts of US policies which suit their purpose. By spurning the

Hamas government, the US, in effect, told Arab leaders that their continuing, often harsh, rule was preferable to democratic elections that might strengthen the hands of local Islamists, extremist or otherwise. In an article in early 2008, entitled *Return to Reason, Mr President*, Khaled al-Maeena, a prominent Saudi journalist, warned president Bush that American foreign policy had 'resulted in all the chaos in the region'. Americans were highly respected, but the US image in most Muslim countries remained abysmal. US support for Israel, 'despite its occupation and suppression of Palestinians, has upset many people'. Al-Maenna appealed to the American president to set the Palestinians free and to insist that Israel had no choice but to withdraw from the West Bank and Gaza—'not to indulge the Palestinians but to save itself'.

But Israel is only part of the reason for Arab rulers not devoting more attention to their domestic problems. The other excuse is Iran, whose challenge to the Arab world will grow in the decades ahead. Iran's primary enemy is Israel. But the more it targets Israel, the greater the tensions and threats between the Jewish and Persian states, and the more Arab leaders will argue that the time is not ripe for the dangerous task of internal reform. So they will have a choice of excuses: Israel; Iran; and Israel versus Iran. The results of the Pew Global Attitudes Project, published in mid-2007, reflected the double whammy—or bonus—of Israel and Iran. Israel was seen as a major threat by overwhelming majorities in Egypt (86 per cent), Jordan (81 per cent), and Lebanon (74 per cent). Ironically, the percentage was lower among Palestinians (60), although Palestinians ranked Israel as the greatest threat, ahead of the US (48 per cent) and Britain (16 per cent). (The survey was conducted before the Hamas takeover of Gaza in June 2007, so the figure for Israel is certain to have increased since then.)

The project found that Israel was not the only cause of concern. Some 52 per cent of Kuwaitis, 46 per cent of Jordanians, 42 per cent of Lebanese, and 27 per cent of Egyptians included Iran among the three biggest threats. In Lebanon, the threat perception of Iran differed dramatically between Christians and Sunni Muslims (56 and 59 per cent respectively) on the one hand, and Shia Muslims (a mere 8 per cent) on the other; the latter, in fact, ranked Iran (and Syria) highly as dependable allies. In Egypt, Iran ranked third after Israel and the US in threat perceptions, while the US also figured in the top three threats in Jordan, Kuwait, Morocco, and the Palestinian territories (and topped the list, at 64 per cent, in non-Arab Turkey). The Iranian 'threat', conceivably, offers more justification for resolving the Israeli–Palestinian conflict. The former Palestinian Authority minister Ziad Abu Zayyad commented in 2007 that Iran's increasing influence in the region, and the polarisation between Sunni and Shia Muslims, 'led some Arab countries to conclude that ending the

Palestinian–Israeli conflict would allow them to devote all their resources and energy to confronting the new dangers and threats instead of being preoccupied with the old Arab–Israeli conflict'. The reality, however, is that these states will face an essentially unresolvable Arab/Palestinian–Israeli conflict *and* a growing Iranian threat.

Arab (and Israeli) leaders concerned about Iran's shadow over the region would hardly have been reassured by a report to the US Congressional Committee on Foreign Relations in early 2008, entitled *Chain Reaction: avoiding a nuclear arms race in the Middle East.* The report declared that, despite the earlier US National Intelligence Estimate (NIE) conclusion that Iran had abandoned its nuclear weapons program, Iran continued to enrich uranium, and the program remained 'one of the most serious threats to US interests and Middle East peace'. Any pause was tactical, rather than strategic. Iran already possessed the scientific, technical, and industrial capacity 'eventually to produce nuclear weapons' if it decided to do so. The NIE had judged 'with moderate confidence' that Iran would have enough highly enriched uranium to produce a nuclear weapon between 2010 and 2015. With the motivations for Iran's drive for nuclear weapons unchanged, 'Iran remains unlikely to fully abandon its long-term drive to obtain a nuclear weapon capability.' It was entirely possible that the United States could confront a nuclear-armed or nuclear weapons-capable Iran in the next decade. This would dramatically shift the balance of power between Iran and its three most powerful neighbours—Saudi Arabia, Egypt, and Turkey—possibly sparking 'a regional nuclear arms race'.

How, the report to the congressional committee asked, would Riyadh, Cairo, and Ankara respond if Tehran were to cross the nuclear threshold and acquire nuclear weapons? The answers were chilling. An Iranian nuclear weapon would 'place tremendous pressure on Saudi Arabia to follow suit'. The only factor likely to dissuade the Saudis would be a restored US–Saudi bilateral relationship and a repaired Saudi perception about the reliability of the American security guarantee. Without these, an Iranian bomb would 'almost certainly lead to a Saudi bomb'. Where would the bomb-making expertise come from? The report noted that Pakistan and Saudi Arabia have 'common interests and complementary assets. Pakistan has a nuclear capability and limited money, while Saudi Arabia has no nuclear capability and virtually unlimited money'.

And if an Iranian bomb led to a Saudi bomb, how would other Arab states react? The key country here is Egypt, which would eye both a nuclear-armed Iran *and* Saudi Arabia with grave suspicion, though for very different reasons. An Iranian bomb would trigger heated debate in Cairo about whether Egypt should pursue nuclear weapons. Two critical considerations for the Egyptians would be Israel's response and Egyptian–US relations. Both Israel and America remain very unpopular with the Egyptian people, but the Egyptian regime has relied on peace with Israel and aid from the United States to maintain its security and its power. Egypt's pursuit of nuclear weapons would destabilise, perhaps topple, the Israeli and American pillars of the Egyptian national security strategy.

As long as peace with Israel and a security relationship with the United States have been in Egypt's interests, the disincentives for an Egyptian nuclear weapons program have outweighed the incentives. That said, the report to the congressional committee warned that the Israeli and Saudi response to a nuclear-armed Iran could 'decisively shape Egypt's response'. Iran's acquisition of nuclear weapons would be a major political and strategic shock to Israel, and the Israeli government would face 'tremendous political pressure to respond in an explicit and bold way' that could be decisive in determining Egypt's reaction. A nuclear-armed Saudi Arabia would challenge Egypt's self-perception as the natural leader of the Arab world. Put bluntly, Saudi oil wealth, control of the 'two holy places' (Mecca and Medina), and ownership of the first 'Arab bomb' might be too much for the Egyptians to stomach. So Iranian nuclear ambitions could, in fact, trigger a four-way arms race: between Iran and Israel; between the Persian and Arab worlds; within the Arab world, principally between Saudi Arabia and Egypt, but possibly also involving Syria and Libya; and between the Arab world and Israel. This was not a pretty thought for anyone interested in Middle East 'peace processes'.

The growing question for Israel and the Arab world is this: do they pose the biggest threat to the other, or do they share a greater common enemy in Iran? If the answer is the latter, can they cooperate against Iran? If, for example, Israel were to undertake a military strike against Iranian nuclear facilities, what would the Arab world do: willingly allow overflight, or denounce publicly while applauding privately? Israel sold arms to Ayatollah Khomeini's Iran to assist the Islamic republic's struggle against largely secular Iraq. Would it cooperate militarily with Saudi Arabia? If Iran is the enemy both of the US and Israel, can it be the friend of the Arab world, or extend its reach beyond Syria, Lebanon, and Hamas?

A worrying element for Sunni Arab leaders is Iran's apparent appeal on the 'Arab street'. The 2007 Pew research, mentioned earlier, showed conflicting feelings in the Arab region towards Iran: it was seen as the third-biggest threat in Egypt, after Israel and the United States; the second-biggest threat in Jordan, behind Israel but ahead of the United States; and the first threat in Kuwait, ahead of Iraq and the United States. In Lebanon, reflecting the religious divide in the country and the strength of the Shia community there, Iran was both the third-closest ally and the third-biggest threat. Among

Palestinians, Iran was ranked as the second-closest ally, behind Saudi Arabia and ahead of Egypt.

The findings of a 2008 Arab public opinion poll conducted by the Anwar Sadat Chair for Peace at the University of Maryland and Zogby International further reflected the divide between 'official' opinion and the 'Arab street' Of the 4000 people surveyed across Egypt, Jordan, Lebanon, Morocco, Saudi Arabia, and the UAE, 44 per cent considered that Iran's acquisition of nuclear weapons would have a positive outcome for the Middle East, against 29 per cent who thought the outcome would be negative, and 12 per cent who said it would not matter. Strikingly, in Saudi Arabia and the UAE, whose leaderships are deeply uneasy about Iranian ambitions, the positive-outcome percentages were 73 and 51 respectively. Asked the likely targets of a nuclear-armed Iran, only 8 per cent of respondents said Arab states, against 31 per cent who nominated Israel. A plurality (45 per cent) believed that Iran would not use nuclear weapons, but that they would help the country increase its regional and global influence.

The relaxed attitude in the 'Arab street' notwithstanding, comments by three Arab speakers in early 2008 at a forum on 'Iran on the Horizon', organised by the Middle East Institute in Washington, reflected deep unease about Iran. Dr. Wahid Hashim, associate professor of political science at King Abdul Aziz University in Jeddah, told the gathering:

There is a fever in the area — anti-America and anti-Israel — and Iran is the only knight who will stand up to America. That is why many people support the Iranians. I was very surprised to see Sunnis naming themselves after Hassan Nasrallah.[†] ... In Egypt and Saudi Arabia and elsewhere, people are supporting Hizballah, [they] are supporting Iran against America and Israel, because of the Iranian position against the Israelis.

Iran, he added, would develop the Shi'ite bomb, which 'has to be followed by the so-called Arab nuclear bomb in order to have a balance of power in the region'.

Another speaker, Ibtisam al-Kitbi, assistant professor of political science at the United Arab Emirates University, said that, in the wake of the Iraq disaster, American policies were seen more as being a part of the problem of regional instability than as part of the solution. The United States had been the main guarantor of UAE security, but the administration had 'lost its credibility and sense of wisdom' through the

---

[†] The Lebanese Hizballah leader. In the 2008 University of Maryland/Zogby International poll, 26 per cent of respondents nominated Nasrallah as their most admired world leader, ahead of Syria's Bashar al-Assad (16 per cent) and Iranian President Mahmoud Ahmadinejad (10 per cent). Osama bin Laden came in sixth place, with 6 per cent of the vote.

invasion of and failure in Iraq. The UAE could not be seen to be supporting US policies. Iran had mobilised Arab public opinion in opposing Israel and the United States, winning 'sympathy, if not support'. Iran's size, geographically and demographically, its proximity and military power, were crucial issues for the UAE. So, too, was the fact that, according to the Iranian consulate in Dubai, some 400,000 Iranians lived in the UAE. They did not necessarily support Teheran's policies, but were a 'source of major and permanent political and stability concern for the UAE'. With an estimated 10,000 Iranian firms operating in the UAE, the country was Iran's biggest trading partner in the region, a factor of potential significance if threats of further sanctions against Iran were implemented. Iran, she said, was determined to acquire the bomb to advance its 'hegemony in the region'.

Dr. Sami al-Faraj, president of the Kuwait Centre for Strategic Studies, argued that it was very easy for Iran to be the hegemon 'on the cheap' in the Gulf. It had hurt US policies in Iraq, in Lebanon, and in Palestine. How could the Arabs realistically talk about two Palestinian states, one Islamic, one secular, as some had done after Hamas' takeover of Gaza? Settling the problems of Iraq and Lebanon and Syria, and the Palestinian questions, would erode US influence and enhance Iran's. Iran could use terrorism to become the paramount power on the cheap. It could use war. It could use coercive means.

It could use the treatment of Shi'ite citizens in the predominantly Sunni Gulf states. It could use mishaps in Iraq in order to create havoc and a refugee problem. Al-Faraj warned against allowing Iran to develop a technological edge, in addition to its size and population. Iran already had 'all the elements of hegemony. Add to that finance and technology and that is it.'

The Arab world does not know how to deal with Iran. Its theological connections through the Shia majorities in Iraq and Bahrain, the Shia plurality in Lebanon, and significant Shia communities in Yemen, Kuwait, and Saudi Arabia's main oilfields, gives it a valuable entré. Add to this Iran's championing of the fight against Israel through the Shia Hizballah in Lebanon and the Sunni Hamas in the Palestinian areas, and the problem for Arab Sunni leaders sharpens. In public perception, they are seen as weak-kneed. Saudi, Egyptian, and Jordanian leaders have all publicly warned against Iranian ambitions. They boycotted the 2008 Arab Summit in Damascus to protest Syria's close ties with Teheran. This meant that they did not hear at first hand a plea from the Libyan leader and newly minted Arab 'moderate', Muammar Gaddafi, for improved ties with Iran. Perhaps comforted by Libya's geographic distance, Gaddafi urged his fellow Arabs not to turn Iran into an enemy. He urged the UAE to seek a peaceful resolution with Iran over the three Gulf islands claimed by the UAE but occupied by Iran. 'Are these islands the only thing we have lost?' he asked. The question was clearly rhetorical, for he answered that 'Arab dignity, the Arab future, and the past have been lost'.

But as much as Israel–Palestine and Iran serve the cause of many Arab leaders, the Arabs also have long provided a ready excuse for Israel, which cites Arab militarism as the justification for its own. What else explained its development from the 1950s of a nuclear weapons arsenal? What else explained 'tiny' Israel's extensive arms industry, which in 2007 made it the world's fourth-largest arms exporter? Hiding behind the fig leaf of there being no partner for peace, Israel constantly claimed the moral high ground. But the claiming of other high ground in the West Bank for continuing settlement activity has long been part of the reason that Israel felt threatened. Israel and its die-hard supporters cling to the mantra that the problems of peacemaking lie all with the other side. Yet, for more than 40 years, Palestinians have witnessed the relentless alienation of the very West Bank territory that has to become their nation if the two-state solution, to which Israel nominally subscribes, is to have any chance.

There is a remarkable dismissiveness about settlements by some pro-Israelis. Take, for instance, one of Israel's most ardent and articulate supporters, Alan Dershowitz. In *The Case for Israel*, Dershowitz wrote that, as Arab and Palestinian hostility to Israel pre-dated settlements, they could not be 'the real barrier to peace'. Rather, this was 'the unwillingness of many Palestinians, and many Palestinian terrorist groups and nations, to accept the existence of a Jewish state in any part of Palestine'. This airbrushes the fact that when Israel and the Palestinian Liberation Organisation, under Yasser Arafat, formally recognised each other through the 1993 Oslo Accords, laying the groundwork for a two-state solution, Israel's response was to allow a doubling of the settler numbers in the West Bank over the following decade. Israeli Bureau of Statistics data shows that population growth in Israel proper between 2001–05 averaged just on 1.9 per cent a year; yet the West Bank settler population continued to grow by approximately 5 per cent annually. During 2007, the settler population in the West Bank grew by 5 per cent, or 14,000 people, to reach 282,000. This increase occurred against the drum-beat from Israelis, especially after the Hamas takeover of Gaza, about there being no partner for peace on the Palestinian side.

There are no partners, there will be no two-state solution, and there will be no peace. The growing religiosity of the conflict—evidenced by Hamas's rise to power and the increased influence of the religious-right in Israeli politics—makes the ideal of a 'secular' line-on-the-map solution redundant. In mouthing the sentiment of peace, Arab leaders are out of step with their own publics, who they have conditioned to think otherwise. A public opinion poll in 2006, for example, found that 30 per cent of Egyptians, 36 per cent of

Jordanians, and 42 per cent of Saudis believed that the Arabs should continue to fight Israel *even* if it peacefully returned all the remaining territories captured in 1967 (the West Bank and the Golan Heights). The tide of peace-making is running out.

The *Report on Israeli Settlement in the Occupied Territories*, published regularly by the Foundation for Middle East Peace, has commented trenchantly but accurately that, at best, Israel now offers the Palestinians 'a truncated statelet'. At worst, 'it would cede only fragmented, scattered West Bank enclaves'. Either option would foreclose 'a viable Palestinian state and promises periodic, violent Palestinian rebellion'. Israel's settlement policy, the report continued, resulted from 'dysfunctional politics made worse by a pathology of denial and an excessive trust in force'. No less importantly, the policy persisted because 'the indulgent protection of the United States' has enabled Israel to avoid adopting realistic policies needed to protect its long-term security and its identity as a Jewish, democratic state.

As if on cue, Condoleezza Rice told a congressional subcommittee hearing in March 2008 that the US considered the expansion of settlement activity to be inconsistent with Israeli obligations under the road map for peace drawn up by the European Union, Russia, the United Nations, and the United States. Such expansion, she said, was 'certainly not helpful to the peace process'. Rice should know, better than most, that successive Israeli government care not one jot what US administrations say about settlements. Israelis will build settlements when and how they see fit. If the US wishes to withhold a few dollars to ensure that no US money is tainted, so be it. There is no risk to the macro-levels of US funding to Israel, which naturally frees Israeli funds for the task of settlement-building.

The Oslo process initiated in 1993 was intended to mark the end of 'Greater Israel' and Palestinian violence. Tragically, it did neither. It is true that Oslo did not expressly forbid settlements, but it did call for the 'integrity and status' of the West Bank and the Gaza Strip to be preserved as the parties inched towards final negotiations. We can only wonder how an extra 10,000-or-so Israeli settlers heading towards the West Bank each year after Oslo was meant to fit into this scenario. Israeli supporters have argued that as the Palestinians kept negotiating after 1993, settlement activity notwithstanding, they cannot have been all that important. By the same grubby logic, we might note that Israel continued to negotiate, albeit fitfully, despite Palestinian terrorist attacks in the period after 1993. So what was the big deal about terrorism?

Israel's defenders are right to argue the unfairness of blaming all the woes of the Arab and Islamic worlds on the unresolved Israeli–Palestinian conflict. The conflict is a good excuse, but a bad justification for many of those shortcomings. Fixing it would not make the problems go away. But as much as Israeli bad behaviour suits the needs of Arab rulers, so too do the threats coming from the Arab world provide a rationale for this behaviour. The threats may not always be quite as existential as Israeli leaders make out. Here, paradoxically, Iranian President Mahmud Ahmadinejad has done Israel a great favour by speaking in strident, unequivocal tones of his intention to destroy the Jewish state. What does it matter whether this intent is shared by the Iranian leadership? What if it is mere bombast? What if it is utterly unrealistic in practical terms? It is, in its own bizarre way, good news for Israeli leaders. How can anyone expect Israel to behave in a gentlemanly fashion when it is under such dire threat?

In looking at the grinding relationship between Israelis and Palestinians, and their willingness to give each other reason, though not justification, for bad behaviour, the similarities of mindset are noteworthy. Ultra-conservative attitudes towards women are by no means confined to Islam or the Arab world. Is there really such a huge philosophical difference between the Muslim veil and the wig worn by ultra-orthodox Jewish women outside the home? Some Muslim Arab men pointedly refuse any physical contact, include hand-shaking, with women; so do ultra-orthodox Jewish men. Both religious belief and social attitudes are much closer in motivation and action than many would care to admit. If extremist Muslims deny Israel's right to exist, their Jewish counterparts articulate equally strong attitudes against the notion of a Palestinian state. If extremist Palestinians or others threaten 'to drive the Jews into the sea', extremist Jews also seek to expel the Palestinians. Their destination may be the desert rather than the ocean, but the intent is similar.

Ethnic cleansing, relocation, or the gentler euphemism of 'transfer', has bobbed around in Israeli thinking since long before the creation of the modern state. The roll-call of Israeli notables hankering after the idea included Ben-Gurion, Yitzhak Rabin, and Ariel Sharon. One of its most energetic and vulgar advocates has been Avigdor Lieberman, founder of the Yisrael Beytenu (Israel is Our Home) party, which won 11 seat in Israel's 2006 election. Among Lieberman's contributions to a resolution of the Israeli–Palestinian conflict was a description of Israel's Arab citizens, who make up nearly 20 per cent of the country's total population, as its 'number one problem'; these citizens, he said, should 'take their bundles and get lost', and Palestinian prisoners held by Israel should be driven to the Dead Sea and drowned. Lieberman also called for the execution of any Arab Israeli parliamentarian who meets with representatives of the Hamas-led Palestinian government. These utterings cannot be dismissed out of hand. For a time, Lieberman was Israel's deputy prime minister and its minister for strategic affairs. An opinion poll published in September 2006 placed him second, after Benjamin Netanyahu, as the preferred Israeli prime minister.

In 1869, the French general Eugene Daumas, at one time director of Arab affairs in Algeria, wrote in *La Vie Arabe* (*Arab Life*) that, while Europeans were striding ahead, Arabs were moving 'neither forward nor backward'. He doubted whether they would ever stride ahead. For Daumas, and for many of his ilk, there was little recognition of shared pasts, of the contribution of the Arab and Islamic worlds to the one in which he lived and prospered. We should note, too, that European 'striding ahead' took a terrible toll on many, destroying the lives of millions in Africa and Asia, and in Europe itself producing two cataclysmic wars that added tens of millions to the death toll. Europeans might have had a civilising mission, but the package included syphilis and mass murder, as well as beads and mirrors.

The peculiar evil of the Holocaust, a distinctly European phenomenon, imposed a heavy price upon the Arab world, at least in Arab eyes. Yet whatever the blame that can be laid at others' feet, whatever the explanations offered for Arab inaction and failures, and the lack of 'striding ahead,' Arab leaders have not been marionettes. They have chosen to pursue the policies they have; they have opted to rule the way they do. They have made authoritarianism and corruption a way of life. Israel is a fig leaf, not a justification. Future historians will debate just when the Israeli–Palestinian conflict reached a 'tipping point' on its journey from nationalist to religious struggle. But that is what it has become, that is what it will remain, and that is what will make it increasingly insoluble.

Like an endlessly running conveyor belt, the Israeli–Palestinian conflict will continue to provide Arab leaders with a rationale for the problems of their creaking fiefdoms. At times, the perennial problem of Palestine and the imminent danger of Iran will make them uncomfortable. But it will also make them thankful.

CHAPTER SIX

With Friends Like These …

Whatever the world's major actors think of the Arab world, they know it is good for two things—keeping their cars on the road, and their arms factories humming. The region's insatiable appetite for military ware, hard or soft, is the dream of American, European and, indeed, Asian manufacturers. Their factories run on Middle Eastern oil which, of course, must be paid for. What better way to close the circle than to sell arms to Arab governments? The funds that flow out for oil then flow back for arms purchases. Everyone's a winner—so long as they are Arab or foreign governments, arms makers, or arms 'consumers'.

The view is less rosy for anyone concerned that the Middle East is a world leader in militarisation; that its governments spend more on arms as a percentage both of total national income and imports than any others; and that it is home to the world's most intractable conflict, which leaches into other uncertainty and bloodshed.

And that the billions of dollars spent on arms means that billions of dollars are not spent on meeting the everyday needs of populations growing at dizzying rates.

Many Middle Eastern states appear dysfunctional. The lucky ones have oil to cover their mistakes, to buy off their opponents, or to purchase the wherewithal to silence them. The oil and gas riches of states such as Kuwait, Qatar, and the UAE give their leaders an open-ended get-out-of-jail card. Still, they might take note of Saudi Arabia. Its fabulous oil wealth has not prevented a collapse in per-capita income in the space of one generation. Arab elites will go on enjoying lavish lifestyles, hoping that 'trickledown' will buy domestic quiescence. But with a careful eye on their own and their nation's security, and with the sharpening divide between the Arab and Persian worlds, they will frequent the international arms bazaar more than ever. Arms manufacturers and traders will continue to enjoy good times. Middle men, often 'middle princes', will go on doing very nicely, peace or war making little difference to their bank balances.

Middle Eastern regimes, nations, and peoples have good reason for their insecurity. Borders are often artificial—the product of neat colonial minds, not geographic or human realities. Tensions between the Arab and Persian worlds, brutally illustrated in eight years of war in the 1980s between Iraq under Saddam Hussein and Iran under Ayatollah Khomeini, add to longstanding

Israeli–Arab hostility and an array of Arab–Arab disputes, including those between Libya and Tunisia, Libya and Egypt, Egypt and the Sudan, Algeria and Morocco, Saudi Arabia and Yemen and, most spectacularly in recent times, Iraq and Kuwait. Profound ideological, religious, and ethnic divisions have produced civil wars in Yemen and Lebanon, and gruesome violence in the Sudan. The inherent suspicions and insecurities of authoritarian leaders drive them to lavish funds on military purchases. These are aimed at protecting their own privileged position as much as the state.

The last 'classic' Arab–Israeli war erupted as long ago as 1973. Yet, since then, Israel has fought two wars with and in Lebanon; there have been two major Palestinian–Israeli eruptions; and the Gulf War of 1990–91 ended Saddam Hussein's expansionist ambitions in Kuwait, while the 2003 US invasion of Iraq ended his life. Clearly, the Middle East offers rich opportunities for both conventional and non-conventional fighting (the latter now fashionably termed 'asymmetric' conflict). Given the mix of factors and animosities at work, it is little wonder that for the last two decades of the twentieth century, the Middle East was the world's most highly militarised region. Military expenditure was $60 billion in 1991. That figure was not reached again until 2004. In 2005, total expenditure reached $70 billion, and it was slightly higher the following year. In the decade to 2004, military spending worldwide increased by an average of

23 per cent; in the Middle East, it rose by 40 per cent. Between 2002–05, Middle East nations accounted for nearly 55 per cent of total arms deliveries to the world's developing nations, spending around $44 billion in the process. The main suppliers were the United States, the United Kingdom, and France. The broader 'Middle East' (if we include Iran) has some three million men (mostly) under arms. Gross numbers though, compounded by the difficulty of reliable statistics (the most valuable data comes from the US Congressional Research Service and the Stockholm International Peace Research Institute) are a poor pointer to military ability. The issue of the quality of men and materiel points to the reality that (Iran aside) only Israel and Egypt, the greatest beneficiaries of US military assistance, have the capacity to fight a sustained conventional conflict.

Events in recent years in Iraq, Lebanon, and elsewhere have been traumatic. Yet they largely continue the pattern of the past century, in which local, national, and international factors shaped and reshaped the contours of the Middle East. World War I drove the final nail into the coffin of the Ottoman Empire, fuelling a deadly cocktail of Jewish, Arab, and Palestinian nationalism; the Nazi destruction of European Jewry and the guilt this rightly engendered in Europe and beyond made Israel's creation inevitable, despite the equally inevitable hostility of the Arab world; Israel's very military successes turned it from a noble cause into an occupier and coloniser;

and the emergence of the US as the dominant external power drew wary support from key Arab states such as Saudi Arabia, Egypt, and indeed Syria in the first war against Saddam Hussein. This evaporated in the US invasion of Iraq in 2003, which had the singular effect of empowering Persian Iran in the Arab heartland, and fuelling the Shia–Sunni divide.

Against this backdrop, two points follow. The first is that the Middle East will be the scene of more war. Whether it is conventional or asymmetrical, it will come. Whether it is conventional or nuclear, it will come. Whether it is Israeli–Syrian, Israeli–Iranian, Israeli–Arab, Arab–Iranian, or Arab–Arab, it will come. Whether it is in 2010, 2020, or 2040, or any time in between, it will come. Peace is a stranger in the Middle East — not because Arabs or Israelis or, further afield, Iranians are programmed by some mysterious force to kill each other or their own, but because a deadly mix of historical grievance, human failing, and human stupidity has primed them to do just that. Add to the mix foreign meddling, driven by the pragmatic desire for oil, the theological pull of the 'Holy Land', and the strategic games that all countries like to play, and the wick is primed constantly. All that is needed is the spark.

The second point involves a paradox. The very failure of American policy in Iraq has made the US more important to so-called moderate Arab nations. If, in 2003, president Bush and defence secretary Rumsfeld had declared, 'We are going to war in Iraq because our strategic interests will be best served by increasing Iran's reach into the Arab world, scareing the Saudis, Egyptians, and a few others witless, and making us more indispensable', they would have been much closer to the mark than lying about weapons of mass destruction or waffling about democratising the Arab world. In the years ahead, the Israeli–Palestinian conflict will not be resolved peacefully; Iran will continue to pursue nuclear weapons and strengthen its reach in the Arab world; key Arab states will seek weapons of mass destruction; and Iraq will remain a mess. Add to this the growing demographic and social pressures within many Arab states (which may well sharpen the appeal of extremist ideologies), and the ageing of authoritarian Arab leaders (whose success should be seen in their capacity to hang on to power rather than their nation-building capacities), and the next 20 years are likely to make the last look rosy by comparison.

Two main groups will be keen to see more war in the Middle East. The first are believers in the apocalyptic message of Judeo–Christian–Muslim thought. The second group have a more prosaic interest: they sell arms. For them, the Middle East is a heaven-sent market and testing ground. The more oil it produces and the nastier the neighbourhood, the better for business. Both groups have cause for optimism, as the prospects for more war are good—very good. It might seem unfair to blame future wars on religious belief. The actual causes superficially may well be more mundane: contested boundaries, water and other precious resources, political ambitions, the need to pursue or protect national honour. But God will be lurking. The judgement-day philosophy in Judaism, Christianity, and Islam paves the way for redemption of those in the right camp. Choose your religion and keep your fingers crossed for war. What better battleground than the Middle East, where so many have been smote in the name of God?

While the continuing mess in Iraq should be an embarrassment to American political leaders, it hardly changes US interests in the region. For the past half-century, these interests have rested on the twin pillars of protecting oil supplies and the state of Israel. The enemies were various: communism represented by the Soviet Union; right-wing Arab regimes not to Washington's liking — exemplified by Libya's Colonel Gaddafi until his 'redemption'; state socialists such as Saddam Hussein and Syria's Hafez al-Assad; and 'nationalist' organisations such as the Palestinian Liberation Organisation under Yasser Arafat. More recently, with the growth of disparate organisations such as al-Qaeda and more focused ones like Hizballah and Hamas, the enemies have assumed an increasingly non-state flavour. Yet this will do little to shift US interests in the decades to come. They will remain focused on oil and Israel, underpinned by the rather bizarre notion that the best reward for peacemaking is to build war-making capacity.

Between 2002–07, US aid to Middle Eastern states, excluding Iraq, totalled $36 billion. Of this, Israel received just under $17 billion; Egypt, $11 billion. These two countries therefore accounted for nearly 80 per cent of the total US aid effort. Of the amounts they received, just under $22 billion, or nearly 80 per cent, was in the form of military equipment or training. American policy of underpinning peace with even more weaponry is akin to providing a lifetime's supply of cigarettes to someone who gives up smoking. US reliance on military bounty in its engagement with the Middle East is striking. In the 30 years to 2001, for example, the US allocated almost $145 billion to Middle Eastern states. Over 90 per cent of this went to Israel and Egypt. Of Israel's share, 64 per cent was military; Egypt's, 53 per cent. The third-largest recipient, Jordan, received just over $4.5 billion in total, with economic aid outweighing military assistance. The happy situation for US arms manufacturers is that every transfer to Israel creates more demand from the Arab states, and vice versa. The spiral effect is very good for business.

Such largesse comes with carrots and sticks. Egyptian support for the US in 1991 in expelling Saddam Hussein from Kuwait led to the cancellation of a military debt worth nearly $7 billion. Meanwhile, aid to Jordan was cut by nearly 75 per cent as punishment for King Hussein's unwillingness to follow the Egyptian lead.

In late 2003, the US announced a reduction of $290 million in loan guarantees to Israel. This was intended to put pressure on Israel over its settlement activity in the occupied West Bank and the construction of the security barrier through Palestinian areas beyond Israel's 1967 border. As usual, this slap on the wrist had little effect on Israeli policy.

By any reasonable measure, the Middle East represents an arms dealer's dream. According to Congressional Research Service data, the main Middle Eastern purchasers of US arms between 2002–05 were Egypt, Saudi Arabia, and Israel. The principal buyers of Russian arms were Iran, Syria, Yemen, Libya, and Israel. Purchasers of Chinese arms were Egypt, Iran, and Saudi Arabia. Between 1998 and 2005, arms deliveries to all 'developing nations' totalled $135 billion, of which Saudi Arabia ($50 billion), the UAE ($11 billion), Egypt ($10 billion), and Israel ($9 billion) accounted for 60 per cent. The US held a strong place, but competition was keen, especially from Western European suppliers, who dominated the UAE and Saudi markets. The US supplied just under 90 per cent of deliveries to Egypt and Israel, and 34 per cent to Saudi Arabia. In 2005, according to data compiled by the Stockholm International Peace Research Institute (SIPRI), 40 US firms accounted for 63 per cent of the worldwide arms sales (totalling $290 billion), followed by West European and then Russian companies. SIPRI noted that Russia's limited internal market had led to an arms industry heavily dependent on exports. The Congressional Research Service commented that Russia was a continuing strong competitor. Its most significant arms-transfer agreements continued to be with China and India. But, through 'creative financing and payment options' and other means, it had worked to expand prospects elsewhere, including the Middle East.

Who or what is all this weaponry meant to deter? Both for the Arab world and Israel, an Iran that is growing in strength is an obvious answer. Gal Luft and Anne Korin of the Institute for the Analysis of Global Security have written that feeble Sunni Gulf monarchies 'have become arms-crazed as never before' because of the Sunni–Shia divide: 'Awash in petrodollars, and fearing the rise of Shi'ite Iran, they have embarked on a military shopping spree, acquiring top-of-the-line fighter aircraft, cruise missiles, attack helicopters, missile-defense batteries, and hundreds of modern tanks.' The Dubai-based Gulf Research Centre has reported that the six members of the 'Cooperation Council of the Arab States of the Gulf', Saudi Arabia, Kuwait, Bahrain, Qatar, the UAE, and Oman (more commonly known as the Gulf Cooperation Council, or GCC) signed 13 deals worth $35 billion, mostly with Western countries, in 2006.

The 'negative influences' of al-Qaeda, Hizballah, Syria, and Iran were cited by Condoleeza Rice in mid-

2007 for a revamped ten-year US military assistance package largely made up of $20 billion worth of precision-guided bombs, aircraft upgrades, new warships, and other equipment to Saudi Arabia; $13 billion worth to Egypt; and $30 billion to Israel. The package, said Rice, would add to Israel's ability to defend itself, and bolster Egyptian and Saudi resolve to confronting 'the threat of radicalism and cement their respective roles as regional leaders'.

Anthony Cordesman, a keen scholar of Middle Eastern strategic issues, defended the US move, arguing that the success of Israel's peace with Egypt and Jordan was 'heavily dependent on American military aid to Egypt'. Israel also faced 'new asymmetric threats' from Iran, Syria, and Hizballah, and had to deal with the growing possibility of an Iranian nuclear threat to its very existence. Helping Israel deal with conventional threats freed 'it to deal with those other threats on its own', producing far more stability in the region. Washington, Cordesman continued, could not and should not try to bring security to the Gulf without allies. Saudi Arabia was the only meaningful military power there that could 'help deter and contain a steadily more aggressive Iran'. Sales would take place 'with or without the United States—from Europe, Russia, or China'. Other proponents of the US move likened such sales to renting a motor vehicle. If the US did not provide the service, others ('Europcar' perhaps) would.

Israel, certainly, has very real, legitimate concerns about the Arab world and Iran. The Hizballah missile threat will expand both in quantity and in quality, bringing major Israeli cities within reach of attack. With Syria's co-operation, Iranian support and technology is transforming Hizballah from a largely manageable border irritant to a strategic, though not existential, threat. The mix of military capability and rhetoric (both Hizballah's and Iranian) should give Israelis sleepless nights. But the lesson from Iraq is that the 'cure' can be worse than the 'ailment'. Those who warn of the perils of 'appeasement' of Iran might do well to study a little history — clearly something overlooked in the ideologically bound decision to invade Iraq and get Saddam. They might note Professor Fred Halliday's observation that, in 'today's tense times, it is worth remembering that the last occasion Iran invaded a foreign country was when Shad Nader Shah occupied Delhi in 1736, a non-aggression record of nearly three centuries which no other significant state in the world, even including Scandinavia, can claim'. The Iran issue does involve more than just the threat of open warfare. Iran can meddle and exercise an unwelcome influence — from an American, Israel, and Sunni Arab perspective — without engaging in outright invasion.

Israelis are fond of remarking that 'even paranoiacs have enemies'. It would be ludicrous to suggest that any state, Middle Eastern or otherwise, does not have legitimate security needs requiring some degree of military preparedness. But this should not mask the question of whether the tens of billions of dollars spent on arms each year makes the Middle East more secure, and the world safer. Cordesman has commented that defence contractors 'exist to sell regardless of need or merit'. The result is a weapons-satiated Middle East. Does this help or hinder security, both regionally and more broadly? How does it help social, economic, and political progress? It is all too easy to give or to sell more weapons. But then it was all too easy to easy to support Saddam Hussein against Ayatollah Khomeini's Iran; it was equally 'logical' to help the anti-Soviet pre-Taliban mujahideen in Afghanistan. The Middle East provides plentiful opportunity for short-term gain and long-term pain.

Yet, in dramatically shifting the old strategic 'balance', the US has done itself a curious favour. If conservative Sunni Arab states are alarmed about Iran's theological and imperial ambitions, the country to look to for protection is the United States itself. American reasons for going to war in Iraq may have been false, driven by hubris and ideological blindness, and the Iraq quagmire may have fuelled Iranian ambitions, but US interests in protecting Israel and oil supplies have not changed. If anything, the US is even more indispensable to conservative Arab monarchies and republics, precisely because of the mess and instability it has helped to create.

Despite American military largesse, these states cannot protect themselves. Cordesman wrote caustically in 2005 that, unless radical shifts took place in virtually every aspect, talk about regional military security concepts was 'a well meaning fantasy'. The problem was 'the lack of any realistic collective decision to act'.

But the US is on the nose; Iraq is just the latest manifestation. Its problem goes much deeper, to the heart of its involvement with the Arab world. This problem is Israel or, more precisely, the widespread view in the Arab world that there is little to distinguish US policy from Israeli policy. In the 2008 University of Maryland/ Zoby International poll, 83 per cent of respondents had an unfavourable opinion of the US (64 per cent, 'very unfavourable'). Fifty per cent of respondents preferred France, Germany, or China as the world's only superpower (with the US coming fourth at 8 per cent). Only 7 per cent of those polled sympathised with al-Qaeda because it sought to create an Islamic state, yet 30 per cent sympathised with its confronting the United States. The US-equals-Israel equation was mirrored by the fact that 95 per cent of respondents believed that Israel posed the biggest threat to them, only marginally ahead of the US at 88 per cent. In stark contrast, the next-biggest threat was Iran at 7 per cent.

The US–Israel relationship damages America's image, and its room for manoeuvre and influence across the Arab world. Yet the US–Israeli military relationship is extraordinary indeed in the favoured treatment that Israel receives over Arab mendicants, especially Egypt. Despite the long-standing Israeli–Egyptian peace treaty, which has been carefully respected by Egypt despite Israeli lamentations of a 'cold peace', US military and other assistance to Egypt is carefully doled out, depending on Egyptian good behaviour and 'reform' efforts. Israel, in the measured words of the Congressional Research Service, receives benefits 'that may not be available to other countries'. It can use US military assistance for research and development in the United States, and can spend a percentage of US funds on military purchases in Israel itself. All US foreign assistance earmarked for Israel 'is delivered in the first 30 days of the fiscal year.' Other recipients, including Egypt, normally receive their aid in 'staggered instalments at varying times'. In becoming the world's fourth-largest arms exporter, Israel has become a significant supplier of defence products to the United States. Their value is roughly half the $2 billion-plus that Israel receives each year in US military assistance.

Cordesman has written that the Arab–Israeli conflict has long been a force that threatens Saudi–US security relations. 'Poll after poll has shown that there is no greater source of hostility to the United States than the Arab and Islamic perception that it is a co-belligerent with Israel'. What, if anything can the US do about this? The obvious answer is to promote an equitable, viable resolution of the Israeli–Palestinian conflict, but the chances of that happening are remote. This is not merely because of the fracture in Palestinian society. The idea always demanded a level of idealism, pragmatism, and determination, which is precisely what remains seriously lacking on both sides. The perfect excuse for inaction always lay in the other's bad behaviour—and neither side has disappointed in this regard. The longer this remains the case, the more opportunity there is for Iran to promote itself as the only true friend of the Palestinians, accusing 'moderate' Arab leaders of having 'sold out' to the United States. In taking the fight to Israel, a popular cause on the Arab 'street', Iran is probably also aiming at reducing suspicions in the Sunni world about its Shia outreach activities.

The US faces a curious reality in its dealings with Middle East. The greater the instability, the less secure Israel will be. Yet, depending on the sources of that instability, more Arab governments are likely to seek shelter under a US strategic umbrella. From a US point of view, Middle Eastern instability, while theoretically uncomfortable for Israel, is likely to produce benefits for US relations with key members of the Arab world, and for US arms manufacturers. And the more that authoritarian Arab regimes cosy up to the US for protection, the more likely they are to generate the very domestic discontent that requires American support. If and when this discontent turns violent, US-supplied 'security' hardware can be used against it. US interests are well served by 'security', providing that the 'right' people are there to administer it.

The situation of rising Iranian influence, aided and abetted by the fiasco of US involvement in Iraq, might actually serve US interests, but it will not make Israel any more pliable. That country knows it can (and does) get away with almost anything. But it may well extend US leverage over Egypt, Jordan, and Saudi Arabia, which have led the charge against Iranian influence. Iran cannot compete with Saudi Arabia religiously. A mere 10 per cent of the world's Muslims are Shia, and Saudi Arabia is custodian of two of Islam's three most holy sites (Mecca and Medina, the third being in Israeli-controlled Jerusalem). Saudi Arabia is predominantly Sunni Muslim, but its Shia minority is concentrated in the oil-rich eastern parts of the country, where it makes up some 30 per cent of the locals. Egypt's President Mubarak has warned that, 'Shia are mostly always loyal to Iran and not the country where they live.'

Whatever conservative Sunni leaderships think of the US and, by extension, Israel, they will be on the same side when it comes to a showdown with Iran. A curiosity here is why the US does not work harder to 'de-link' Syria from its Iranian patron. A majority Sunni state ruled by the Alawites (an offshoot of Shi'ism rejected by many Sunni and Shia alike), Syria would seem to be ripe for a creative mix of carrots and sticks. Syria's problem with Israel is no longer the very fact of its existence, but the fact of its continuing occupation of the Golan Heights. The US (and Israeli) default setting of threats and warnings to Syria only drives it deeper into Iran's clutches. To wean Syria away might dramatically limit Iran's capacity for meddling in the Arab world.

The Iranian 'question' leads inevitably to a focus on the Strait of Hormuz, the narrow waterway separating the Persian and Arab worlds, through which some 40 per cent of the world's traded oil moves. Whatever the tensions between the Arab world and Iran, or between the US and its allies and Iran, this waterway will become increasingly important in coming decades. The reason is simple: the world is growing increasingly dependent on Middle Eastern energy. Gulf oil, as a proportion of total world production, is likely to increase to nearly 30 per cent by 2020. By 2025, America, China, Japan, and India could be importing at least three-quarters of their total needs. All four countries are critically dependent on maritime imports—and passage through the Strait of Hormuz. At its most critical juncture, the strait narrows to two 2-mile-wide sea lanes (with another 2-mile buffer) for inbound and outbound traffic. The possibility of local factors—such as contested ownership of three strategically important islands (Abu Musa, Greater Tunb, and Lesser Tunb) all occupied by Iran; disputed oil and gas resources; or wider regional issues flaring, and prompting Iran to threaten passage through the strait or to damage vital oil facilities on the Arab side—will continue to haunt world oil trade. It will be compounded by the uncomfortable reality that as world dependence on Gulf oil increases over the next two decades, so too will reliance on a waterway through which Iran can make safe passage very unsafe. Cordesman has argued that Iran could not close the strait for any length of time. But Gulf states, he wrote,

> are extremely vulnerable to any form of attack on their desalination and coastal power facilities, and precision strikes on critical high-capacity, long-lead time replacement items in energy facilities and power grids ... Even sporadic, low-level attacks on Gulf shipping and facilities, however, could allow Iran to wage a war of intimidation in an effort to pressure its neighbours.

The Middle East's strategic uncertainties, fuelled by the gift to Iran of American involvement in Iraq, will make for strange future bed-mates. Arab leaders, especially those in Saudi Arabia, Jordan, and Egypt, may see off the challenge of Islamist extremism in the short term. But their domestic and regional problems will mount, driven in large part by the Arab world's unsustainable population growth. These leaders will go on resenting American heavy-handedness and its often-blind support for Israel. But they will stay firmly under America's wing. The very instability and uncertainty fuelled by US policies will serve to remind Arab regimes where their best chances of survival lie. If Islam is the last idea standing in the Arab world, America is the ally of last resort.

Iran is emerging as a greater threat than Israel to Arab identity and the wellbeing of authoritarian Arab regimes. Sheik Musa bin Abdulaziz, editor of the Saudi *Al Salafi* magazine, and a self-proclaimed moderate in the Salafi fundamentalist Muslim movement, has described Iran as 'more dangerous than Israel itself,' with a Persian presence in the region being 'the real clash of civilisations'. Israel, Iran, and Saudi Arabia now make up a critical triangle. All three define themselves in starkly religious terms: Israel, as the Jewish state; Iran, the birthplace of Sunni Islam; and Saudi Arabia, the heartland of Shia Islam. All three have a lot to prove: Israel, that it has a legitimate place in an otherwise hostile Arab world; Iran, that, though non-Arab, it is now the only meaningful friend of Palestinian liberation and broader Arab 'resistance' to Israel; and Saudi Arabia, that it can combine religious absolutism with modernism, and that September 11, in which its citizens figured prominently, was an aberration. For different reasons, both Israel and Saudi Arabia have something to fear from Iran. It has existentialist designs on Israel, and a strong strategic and theological distaste for Saudi Arabia. It is no accident that, in a region noted for its arms purchases, the leading buyers in 2005 were Israel and Saudi Arabia.

The US may be the last power standing in the

Middle East; but its old adversary, Russia, is setting out to do what its predecessor, the Soviet Union, also did—make life difficult. This is not just through growing competition in arms sales. It is Russia's habit of taking a contrary stand, whether by means of a marked lack of enthusiasm for America's self-proclaimed mission of democratising the Middle East, a greater preparedness to deal with organisations such as Hamas and Hizballah, or the pursuit of important trade, technical, and arms links with countries (particularly Iran and Syria) with whom the US refuses to deal. In a neat package, Russia not only sold the technology for a long-planned nuclear plant at Bushehr on Iran's south-western coast, but the also the missile system to protect it. Russia is acting in a very 'Soviet' way: ensuring that it is a player, maximising its room for manoeuvre, and limiting US freedom of action. It cannot but be conscious, also, that instability is good for high oil prices. This is bad news for the US economy, but very good news indeed for Russia's. A US or Israeli attack on Iran would likely have a dramatic impact on oil prices, at least in the short term. Not only would Russia claim the moral high ground, but it would also laugh all the way to the bank.

America invaded Iraq ostensibly to protect the world from the threat of weapons of mass destruction. If pre-emption is the basis for future military adventures, the US and its allies are likely to be busy. The US is unlikely to invade Israel, of course—the only Middle Eastern state about whose weapons of mass destruction there is no real doubt. But if the US is serious, a range of other targets should lend themselves. It is not so much that weapons of mass destruction (WMD)—chemical, biological, radiological, or nuclear (CBRN)—are coming back on the agenda. They have never really been off it. As well as Israel, a half-dozen Arab states have developed and used, or at least flirted with, chemical or biological agents.

In addition to Iraq and Iran—the former using chemical weapons both against the Iranians and its own Kurdish and Shia citizens—the list includes Algeria, Egypt, Libya, and Syria. Egypt used chemical weapons when it intervened in the civil war in Yemen in the 1960s, and readied them for possible use in the 1973 Arab–Israeli war. Whatever Iran's current plans, its nuclear ambitions predate the country's Islamist revolution in 1979. The Shah was as susceptible to the appeal of nuclear status as any of his successors. CBRN weapons ambitions have driven missile proliferation, with the usual suspects—the former Soviet Union, France, and the US—helping to provide the wherewithal. Scud missiles have been used by Syria (against Israel), by Iraq (against Iran, Israel, and Saudi Arabia), and by Iran against Iraq.

Although deliberately shrouded in ambiguity, an Israeli air attack near Deir al-Zur in north-eastern Syria in September 2007 seems to have been aimed at a nuclear facility built with North Korean help. The raid also had two other aims: resurrecting then Israeli prime minister Olmert's popularity, whose standing in some opinion polls after the fiasco of the Israeli–Hizballah war in 2006 was less than the margin of error; and sending a message to Iran about Israeli resolve and capability. In the carefully controlled media coverage after the raid, the religious-Zionist *Arutz Sheva* news service crowed that the raid had shaken Iranian (and, by extension, Syrian) confidence in its Russian-made radar and air-defence systems. Iranian officials, it asserted, were questioning the wisdom of a proposed $750 million radar equipment purchase from Russia, given Israel's success in circumventing the system in Syria, 'a tactic that could also enable a successful strike against Iran through Syrian airspace'. Syrian President Bashar al-Assad denied any nuclear weapons ambitions, and claimed to have rejected an offer in 2001 from middlemen acting for the rogue Pakistani nuclear scientist Abdul Qadir Khan, fearing it was an Israeli set-up.

It may seem tragic that Middle Eastern states (including Iran) see CBRN weapons as adding to their defensive (or offensive) credentials. But we need to ask the same question of all states with weapons of mass destruction. If Iran is intent on getting *the* bomb, it will do so. It can cite Israel, its immediate neighbourhood, and the failure of nuclear weapons states to disarm under the Nuclear Non-Proliferation Treaty (NNPT) as good cause. Israel is in the curious position of arguing that Iran should be punished for non-compliance with a treaty that Israel itself has consistently refused to sign. Moreover, Article VI of the NNPT requires parties 'to negotiate in good faith' on nuclear disarmament. Non-nuclear states see this as a specific obligation on the treaty's nuclear 'club' (the US, the USSR/Russia, China, Britain, and France). But the language clearly provides wriggle room. That said, who exactly is France's continuing nuclear deterrent aimed at? Or Britain's? If possession of nuclear weaponry is a matter of national honour for France or other members of the club, why should it be any less so for Iran, located as it is in a much tougher contemporary neighbourhood?

Israel, India, and Pakistan have shown clearly that those outside the club can make their own rules, and that 'international' opprobrium has a short shelf-life. If the US and Europe, in particular, want to demonstrate some degree of consistency in containing the nuclear-weapons genie, why not bring the same pressure to bear on Israel, India, and Pakistan that they do on Iran? If the explanation for the different approach is Ahmadinejad's troublesome tongue, would it not be easier to take him out, rather than the country as a whole? Just as bad for genuine anti-proliferationists is the fact that the US and Australia—ostensibly staunch supporters of the NNPT—both agreed to sell uranium to India (a decision overturned by Australia's new Labor government, elected in late 2007). If the world's largest known source of uranium, Australia, was prepared to sell it to a country that has stood defiantly outside the NNPT while testing nuclear weapons, how can anyone take the treaty seriously, let alone threaten Iran with military punishment for following its neighbour's lead? This is not to justify Iranian actions or a nuclear weapons race in the Arab world or beyond. It is to say that the hypocrisy of key nuclear-weapons states and uranium suppliers has mortally wounded the NNPT, as well as their own moral authority and negotiating strength.

If the US and Israel (with Saudi Arabia in the background) are determined to prevent Iran from become nuclear armed, an attack is inevitable. The tactics of persuasion and economic inducement used to bring North Korea to heel, at least temporarily, will not work. True, the mismanaged Iranian economy is under stress, and the country exhibits sharp social tensions, with younger Iranians resenting the reach of conservative Islam into their lives. But Iran sits on top of around 10 per cent of the world's total known supply of oil; it can play havoc with the 40 per cent of Middle Eastern oil that passes daily through the Strait of Hormuz. US and/ or Israeli bombing could seriously impede its nuclear weapons progress. But this would also harden Iranian resolve, give the project greater popularity among ordinary Iranians, and trigger Iranian retaliation against American and Israeli targets globally. A ground invasion of Iran would be sheer madness.

With Iran nuclear armed, the race among Sunni Arab states to acquire nuclear-weapons capability will be on in earnest. The leading candidates—Egypt and Saudi Arabia—will use the well-trodden rationale of national prestige and self-defence. If they need high levels of conventional weapons against a conventionally armed Iran, as Condoleezza Rice argued they do, why would they not need nuclear weapons against a nuclear-armed Iran? Shifts in domestic Egyptian or Saudi politics could further complicate the picture. Gamal Mubarak is being groomed to succeed his father, but there is no guarantee he will do so. A more nationalistic successor, less amenable to American strictures, could lead Egypt to an aggressive stance towards Israel, in which nuclear armaments would have a 'logical' place. An Islamist takeover in Saudi Arabia might well produce the first 'Arab' bomb, after Iran's Shia one and Pakistan's Sunni weapon. And what of Syria and Libya? If Russia is prepared to sell nuclear technology to Iran, why not to these two countries? Over time, the notion of peaceful nuclear programs in the Middle East is increasingly likely to become an oxymoron.

Since America's use of the atomic bomb against Japan in 1945, nuclear weapons have remained constantly in the arsenal as a deadly, if dormant, threat. Will that be the case in a nuclear-armed Middle East? Who might use them, against whom, and with what impact? In

December 2001, the then Iranian president, Ali Akbar Hashemi Rafsanjani, declared that the 'use of an atomic bomb against Israel would totally destroy Israel, while against the Islamic world [the same weapon] would only cause damage.' Middle Eastern geography and demographics, nonetheless, is a real complication for would-be CBRN users. Given the relatively short distances, it might be easier to achieve surprise than, say, a Russian nuclear-armed missile attack on Washington. But unless weapons with an exceptional degree of accuracy were used, it would hardly be sound tactically for, say, Syria to attack Israel unless it was prepared to sacrifice both the non-Jewish population of Israel, Palestinians in the West Bank and possibly Gaza, and also run the risk of affecting Jordan. Distances between Iran and Israel would help to contain the risk of 'blowback'. But in spite of Rafsanjani's bravado, and despite the animosity between Sunni and Shia Islam, would Iran seriously contemplate an attack that might damage Jerusalem, the Muslim world's third-holiest site? It is doubtful in the extreme. Moreover, the possibility of a 'MAD' (mutually assured destruction) environment might well constrain both Israel and Iran, similar to the way it held the United States and the Soviet Union in check.

Anthony Cordesman has calculated that a nuclear exchange between Israel and Iran, with the former possessing higher-yield and more accurate weapons, could leave between 200,000–800,000 Israelis and between 16 to 28 million Iranians dead in a matter of weeks. His prediction that Israeli recovery would be 'theoretically possible' in population and economic terms, but Iranian recovery 'not possible' in the normal sense of the term, should give trigger-happy leaderships plenty to think about. Yet would the constraints on state actors also apply to non-state ones? The answer is almost certainly no. Al-Qaeda and other extremist organisations have demonstrated more than a passing interest in chemical, biological, and radiological weapons. Prior to 9/11, al-Qaeda in Afghanistan pursued research and development of such weapons, and Osama bin Laden reportedly had two laboratories in competition to 'weaponise' anthrax. al-Qaeda might not succeed, but extremists, Muslim or otherwise, will. Physically, the impact of such biological weapons might not be as devastating as a nuclear explosion. Psychologically, the effect would be profound.

Despite the logistical problems in their use, the appeal of CBRN weapons is obvious. Awareness of a state's capability builds its 'prestige', adding weight both to intimidation and deterrence. These weapons also provide smaller states with the ability to offset conventional threats from larger ones. Given its geographic and personnel limits, Israeli possession of CBRN weapons effectively combines intimidation, deterrence, and equalisation. It is no coincidence that four of the world's seven countries that have not signed the United Nation's Chemical Weapons Convention are Middle Eastern states—Egypt, Iraq, Lebanon, and Syria. (Israel signed the convention in 1993, but has not ratified it.)

There is reason behind the argument of those who claim that supplying Middle Eastern states with conventional weapons is a logical move. The argument has two elements: the market-based or 'rent-a-car' logic (if the US won't supply, the Europeans, Russians, Chinese, or others will); and the hard-to-dispute assertion that the refusal to supply will simply drive Middle Eastern regimes to pursue non-conventional weapons. When it comes to the Middle East, arms-control or export-control regimes will remain a fiction. Cordesman has commented that sub-regional tensions in North Africa, the Gulf, South Asia, and the Arab–Israeli conflict interact in ways 'that may well force all of the major powers in the Middle East to continue their efforts to acquire CBRN weapons and delivery systems, regardless of the nature of the ruling regime'. There were, he said, no current prospects that arms-control and export-control regimes could 'halt the ability of regional states to slowly acquire nuclear weapons and long-range ballistic missiles'. Even if such controls were developed, 'regional states would simply pursue biological weapons and less obvious methods of delivery. As a result, dealing with CBRN threats is likely to be a permanent aspect of the security problems of the Middle East.'

Could it have turned out differently? Might it once have been realistic to imagine that the Arab world could be reformed and demilitarised? What would it have taken? Was the American invasion of Iraq merely the latest chapter in a litany of missteps, epitomised by the notion that the best guarantee of peace was to ensure that countries were well equipped to fight wars? The logic of this might have worked in the past for nations such as Sweden, but the Middle East is no European backwater. The invasion of Iraq, of course, was touted as a way of dealing with WMD. The result, in the decades to come, will be a proliferation in the very weapons that drove an ignorant Bush administration to war. The 'new' Middle East looks uncannily like the old one, only better armed and more dangerous. Bush's departed adviser Karl Rove once commented that 'we're an empire now — we create our own reality'. Iran with the bomb, or a bombed Iran, will make for a very uncomfortable future reality — not just in the Middle East, but well beyond.

CHAPTER SEVEN

Future Shock?

> 'The Arabs, having wallowed in a continuous
> ideological mire for more than two hundred years, find
> themselves surrounded by gloom as they trudge into a
> new century unprepared to deal with its challenges.'
>
> Hilal Khashan *Arabs at the Crossroads*

Imagine it is the year 2020. An Egyptian father and
his son are talking over coffee in a Cairo café. The
son—we'll call him Ramzi—has just announced his
intention to migrate to America, taking his wife and
children. He tells his father that he is determined to
escape the Arab world, and its sickening mix of obscene
wealth and grinding poverty, the endless despair of the
Palestinian–Israeli conflict, the growing threat of nuclear
annihilation. His father, Youssef, is stunned, seeing this
as a both personal and national betrayal. He pleads with

Ramzi to reconsider, pointing out to his son that he has a good job, that he is relatively well-off, and that he has much to offer Egypt and the Arab nation.

Ramzi bristles at the last comment. He is sick of hearing about the Arab nation. There's no such thing, he retorts. There is Egypt, and Tunisia, and Saudi Arabia, and so on — a collection of individual states driven by individual self-interest. These states agree on a few things and disagree on many, even if such disagreement hides behind politeness and platitude. But the notion of an Arab *nation*, Ramzi declares, is a dangerous pretence. Arabs, he argues, always seem to going round in circles. One day it's Arabism, then it's nationalism, then it's reformism, then Islamism, then Arabism again. So many isms, and so little to show for them. Arabs, he says, must learn to move in a straight line.

The conversation itself goes round in circles until Youssef, apparently searching for a fresh line of argument, brings up the work of the famous Arab poet Nizar Qabbani. After the debacle of the 1967 Arab–Israeli war, Youssef notes, Qabbani wrote bitterly, and truthfully, of the disastrous shortcomings of Arab leaders. But Qabbani also wrote of the Arab children, calling them the spring rain, the corn ears of the future, the new generation that would overcome defeat. Youssef adds, pointedly, that these children will not save the Arab world by living in America. Ramzi is quiet for a moment. Then he asks Youssef if he remembers the ending of one of Qabbani's later poems: 'Are we Arabs one big lie?' The two men stare at each other in silence. Finally, Ramzi excuses himself and leaves.

Qabbani's provocative question is one we should all ponder. The Arab footprint on our world is profound indeed—from Islam to astronomy, from oil to Osama bin Laden. But where is the 'Arab world' headed? How well equipped is it to manage the intense demands of the twenty-first century? What remains to bind Arab nations together? Do the threads of shared language, a mostly shared religion, and some overlap of historical experience give an Egyptian peasant and a Saudi prince a common sense of purpose and destiny? How well do these threads equip the Arab states to handle extraordinary population growth and the everyday needs of food and water, education and jobs, let alone big-picture demands linked to global warming and national and regional security? Osama bin Laden is not the cause of the Arab world's malaise. He is a symptom. al-Qaeda's attacks on American targets made him popular on the Arab street. But it is an admiration of despair, by those who see their lives in thrall to others, both nationally and internationally.

This leads to another question. What will it take to 'rescue' the Arab Middle East from a future of growing insecurity and hardship and, by extension, increasing discomfort for the non-Arab world dependent on that region's extraordinary energy riches? For a brief, illusory, moment, Western-style democratisation was marketed, most energetically by American neoconservatives, as the answer. They would free the people of the region, remaking it in their own image and to suit their own interests. 'Regime change', driven by the so-called 'moral clarity' that comes with being the world's single superpower, was the solution. One of its arch proponents, and the self-styled father of neo-conservatism, Norman Podhoretz, wrote that regimes which richly deserved to be overthrown and replaced were not merely the three members of the axis of evil named by president Bush (Iraq, Iran, and North Korea). At a minimum, they included Syria, Lebanon, and 'friends' of America such as the Saudi royal family; Egypt under Hosni Mubarak; and the Palestinian authority, whether 'headed by Arafat of one of his henchmen'. Podhoretz later wrote that the obstacles 'to a benevolent transformation' of the Middle East, military, political or religious, were not insuperable. It was a question of power, resources, skills, and stomach.

But US power mixed with such 'moral clarity' has proved deadly indeed. It has produced more than 4000 US military dead in Iraq (still counting), and possibly hundreds of thousands of dead Iraqi civilians (still counting). It has damaged rather than furthered the cause of Middle East transformation, fuelling support for extremists and giving Iran a helping hand. The US showed itself no better than anyone else — only having more brute force at its disposal. President Bush had once declared that the 20th century ended with a single model of human progress, one that rested on 'free speech and equal justice and religious tolerance'. In pursuing the cause of religious tolerance in the Middle East, who and what did the president have in mind? In Israel, the symbols of the state automatically discount the worth of the 20 per cent of its citizens who are not Jews; in Saudi Arabia, apostates run the risk of being beheaded. President Bush discovered the cause of Palestinian statehood, but made its realisation conditional on Palestinians seeing the world through the US prism when it came to terrorism. Palestinians have carried out acts of cruel, indiscriminate violence. So have their enemies, using the same nationalist argument as cover. President Bush apparently was unaware of Zionist leaders such as Menachem Begin and Yitzhak Shamir, both of whom engaged in terrorist acts to further the creation of Israel, which they later led as its prime minister.

The US and Britain, especially under Tony Blair, liked to talk about success, about winning. In early 2007, Blair declared that 'we will win if we don't apologise for our values'. Leaving aside what values he had in mind (defence industry bribes to Saudi royals, perhaps), what did he mean by win? Osama bin Laden handing himself in; al-Qaeda running up the white flag: only Arabs being killed in Iraq; Hamas disbanding itself and joining the Church of Jesus Christ of Latter-day Saints; or the Iranians announcing the end of theocratic rule and jailing

President Ahmadinejad? If the West and its non-Western friends really want to win against the vicious mindset that al-Qaeda represents, they need to stop acting as its chief recruiting agent. Their often ill-thought-out, ill-pursued policies have delivered short-term gain and long-term pain and, in the process, have debased the values that 'Western civilisation' purports to uphold.

Yet, democratised or not, the Arab world makes for an uncomfortable future for those in the region and beyond. Given the demographic and economic changes taking place about them, will Arab leaders keep the authoritarian cork in indefinitely? We are in an era when information, disinformation, criticism, and embarrassment is only a mouse-click away. If oil is $150 or $200 a barrel, those with this precious resource will have plenty of hush money. But not everyone has oil, and even those with fistfuls of give-away dollars are likely to come under increasing scrutiny from young populations with mostly instant access to a world beyond. There, they see governments being pummelled openly by political rivals, by the media and, indeed, by anyone with an opinion. If and when the corks come out, violently or otherwise, what then? Ironically, the prospect of the current crop of authoritarian leaders being swept away by even less palatable rulers is high indeed.

The 'West' certainly played a part in creating the problems of the Arab world. That much is fact. But the question we should ask is, 'So what'? A sense of Western 'guilt' or Arab 'victimhood' equips no one well for the days ahead. The West, especially America, can interfere and occasionally impose its will, but it cannot 'reform' misogynistic or tribal behaviour. It cannot remake the Arab world in its own image. Iraq is a salutary lesson for Westerners and Arabs alike. And without a dramatic lessening of the West's dependency on Arab oil it will, ironically, increasingly be a courtier of Arab states, not a mender of Arab ways.

But if there is one thing that the West, especially America, can do with a much greater sense of purpose and 'moral clarity', it is to try to remove the one great prop of Arab illiberalism: the Israeli–Palestinian conflict. In the years ahead, Arab leaders will certainly milk the Iranian 'threat' as insurance against domestic and foreign critics. But whatever happens between Iran and Israel, or Iran and the Arab world, the Israeli–Palestinian conflict will continue to 'explain' the all-too-obvious shortcomings of Arab rulers. If the US were really serious about reforming the Arab world, it would bring its great energy and genuine 'moral clarity' to the Israeli–Palestinian conflict. This would not mean 'siding' with the Palestinians, or even liking them, or turning a blind eye to egregious Palestinian behaviour. It would, however, mean abandoning the habit of seeing the Israeli–Palestinian conflict through the prism of the long-gone Cold War, where Israel was a lone American aircraft carrier in a sea of Soviet influence.

In practice, it would mean demanding that the Israelis remove themselves entirely from the occupied West Bank and East Jerusalem. It would mean insisting that Israel relocates its West Bank security barrier to the exact line of the 1967 border. Never mind bleats about 'determining' borders outside the negotiating room. Israel does it as a matter of course; that, in part, is what the settlement movement, helped by all Israeli governments, is about.

If the US were serious, it would tell the Israelis, truthfully, that settlements do not add to their security, but jeopardise it. The US would impose real penalties (financial, security, and otherwise) for Israeli nose-thumbing — not the verbal tut-tutting and meek trimming of loan guarantees that have applied in the past. It would demand that Israel do everything reasonable to give a newborn Palestinian state some chance of survival: this would involve allowing the two halves of the state — the Gaza Strip and the West Bank — to have everyday contact. Israel is not an American satellite and will not always do the US's bidding. But, given the weight of America's political, military, and financial links with the Jewish state, if the US couldn't influence Israeli policy and action when it was essential to do so, the period of the American superpower would clearly have passed.

The US might also swallow hard and deal with those, such as Hamas, that it dislikes intensely and rightly distrusts. After all, Israel's own intelligence services assisted the rise of Hamas, precisely because the Islamists were seen as a useful counterweight to the nationalists of the Palestine Liberation Organisation (PLO) under Yasser Arafat. Later, Israel switched sides, and it and the PLO formally recognised each other. Israel still favours the nationalists of the emasculated Palestinian Authority over the Islamists of Hamas. Whatever the logic in that, locking Hamas up in Gaza and wishing it will go away is not only futile, but also exposes US hypocrisy in applying 'democratic' standards.

The great virtue of a more energetic, genuinely even-handed US approach would be to call the Arab bluff. Without the distraction and the protection of the Israeli–Palestinian conflict, the future Arab world might look very different indeed. The Arab authors of the Arab human development reports were no great friends of Israel. They made it clear that Israeli occupation of Palestinian land threatened the region's security and development. Yet they emphasised, too, that the occupation gave Arab regimes 'a pretext for postponing internal reforms'. It embarrassed Arab reformers by making 'external threats' a higher priority. Calling the Arab bluff would also mean calling the Israeli one. Does it really want a two-state solution, or is it content, if not always comfortable, in sticking with conflict management?

Israel, in turn, would call the Palestinian bluff. A majority of Palestinians polled in 2008 said that Hamas should conduct peace negotiations with Israel, if the latter were prepared to talk. Why not put this to the test? Could Israel not say to the Palestinians: 'You say you need your own state. Here it is, in the Gaza Strip and the West Bank. We have withdrawn entirely from these places; we have shared Jerusalem with you. Now leave us in peace or we will truly destroy you.' Israel would, in effect, give up physical ground to regain moral ground. This may sound a drastic, painful step for Israel to take. But the reality is that, in Gaza, the West Bank, and Jerusalem itself, the ground is already demarcated between Jew and Palestinian. The only time most Israelis go near the West Bank is on military service. Many Israelis are wary of travelling into East Jerusalem, the Old City in particular. Vigorous Israeli settlement activity there notwithstanding, that is where 'Arabs' live. Many Israelis shut their minds to what goes on around them, and get on with their often-comfortable lives. A little less certainty about the US umbrella might encourage them to reflect on the fact that today's 'normalcy' aids and abets Arab dictators.

Public opinion polls have shown consistently that a majority of Israelis and Palestinians support the idea of a two-state solution. They may well have quite different notions about what this would mean in practice, just as the extremists on each side have sharply conflicting ideas of a 'one-state' solution. But is the international community, under American 'direction', really so weak that it cannot drive Israeli and Palestinian leaders to put this into practice? Can 10 million Israelis and Palestinians, highly dependent on the support of that international community, hold it hostage for another 60 years? Why should they be allowed to go on giving the Arab world at large just the excuse it needs to continue its kleptocratic, sclerotic ways?

Some might argue that this is soft, 'liberal' nonsense, which is both unrealistic and indeed dangerous. It is certainly true that there is no magic wand to 'fix' the Israeli–Palestinian conflict. But outsiders can be serious about trying, rather than continuing the charade of 'peace processes'. That is what has brought us to where we are today. Those who baulk at the idea of putting serious pressure on Israel, of giving the Palestinians (led by Hamas or anyone else) a 'take-it-or-leave-it' ultimatum, and of talking to Iran under the mullahtocracy, need to tell us how they see the Middle East in 20 or 30 or 50 years' time, and how they propose to deal with the region's problems and the way these stain the wider world. The most direct way of cleaning up the mess that is today's Middle East is to remove the Israeli–Palestinian conflict as the reason both for Arab prevarication and for foreign meddling.

How much harder life would be for Iran without the Israeli–Palestinian conflict. It is as much a gift to Iranian ambitions as the US overthrow of Saddam Hussein. How much more difficult life would be for Iran's acolytes in the region—the fellow Shia of Hizballah, the Sunnis of

Hamas, or the Alawites of the hardline Syrian regime under Bashar al-Assad. Imagine, too, the possible impact on American relations with the Islamic world as a whole, not just the Muslim nations of the Middle East, if the US acted genuinely for Israeli–Palestinian peace and not as a Pavlovian defender of the Jewish state. Some of Israel's die-hard supporters now suggest that the daily grind of living in one of the world's nastiest neighbourhoods is sapping its sense of purpose. After a prisoner/coffin exchange between Israel and Hizballah in mid-2008, Daniel Pipes, for example, wrote that Israel, 'a once formidable strategic country', had degenerated into a supremely sentimental country, 'where self-absorbed egoism trumps *raison d'être*'. Israelis 'had lost their way'. Given Pipes' track record, he probably believes that Israel beating up on the Palestinians and taking on the Iranians will help the country find its feet again. Israelis would be much better advised to pursue a genuine two-state solution with the Palestinians that would go a long way to crimp Iranian opportunism.

There is no reason why the US should not remain a close friend of Israel, including as a major supplier of arms. There is no reason for America not to continue to protect Israel from the stupidity that sometimes plays out in the United Nations. There is no reason why America cannot also tell the Arab world to 'leave Israel alone, or you'll have do deal with us'. How much more defensible these approaches would be if America could show the stomach to demand real concessions from Israel, and show that the US was no longer prepared to tolerate conflict-management as a substitute for conflict-resolution.

None of this is likely to happen, of course. That would be as much a figment of the imagination as the fictitious conversation that opens this chapter. It would require considerably more courage and consistency than we have seen before. It would require American presidents to break the addiction of declaring undying support for Israel, and then feign surprise and hurt when their credentials for acting even-handedly are questioned. For 60 years, the region has gone round in circles, with peace processes that often are little more than figments of the official imagination. For 60 years, Arab governments have been able to excuse their shortcomings by pointing the finger at Israel, with 'reform' and progress in the Arab world a convenient hostage to the Israeli–Palestinian conflict.

The West will continue to guzzle Arab oil, to wring its hands over the unresolved Israeli–Palestinian conflict, to fret about Iran, and to lament the problems of the Arab world, while ensuring that no arms sales go unclosed. There should be no surprise about this, just as there is no real mystery about the Arab world. Perhaps the real problem with that world—past, present, and future—is that it too closely mirrors the shortsightedness and hypocrisies of our own. Maybe we should just accept these all-too-human failings. Still, when it comes to the Middle

East, the stakes are high indeed. The third Arab Human Development Report predicted a possible future for the region ranging from hopeful to catastrophic. We seem, like a rudderless ocean liner, to be headed for the latter.

Is hope at hand in the form of a new US administration under president Barack Obama? Only the most optimistic, or naïve, will believe in this possibility. True, the new president's rhetoric may help to scrape off the deep layers of tarnish on America's image, in the Arab world and more broadly. But the 'change' is likely to be one more of style than substance. Those who believe that the Obama presidency will mark a dramatic turning point in how the US deals with Israel and the broader Middle East could be sorely disappointed. The promised withdrawal of the bulk of US combat forces from Iraq may fix the worst of the Iraqi problem for America; it may do very little to fix the Iraqi problem for Iraqis or the wider region. The catastrophe of the Bush administration's policy has spawned a life of its own—irrespective of who sits in the oval office. US boots on the ground seem increasingly irrelevant to the sectarian fracture that represents contemporary Iraq and the opportunities there for Iranian sway.

In the lead-up to his historic victory, Obama declared that within ten years he would cut America's dependency on Middle Eastern oil. This pledge was predicated on a dramatic increase in domestic renewable energy. If achieved, it would certainly worry the Saudis and the other oil-rich Gulf kingdoms — not because of a loss of oil sales to America, however. These would quickly be made up elsewhere, especially in China and India. Rather, America's oil thirst drove it to provide a strategic umbrella for the Arab monarchies in the Gulf.

Freed of its need for Arab oil, would America fold the umbrella and take it home, or at least allow only Israel to snuggle under it? Logic says it would. But those Arab states potentially affected should not lose too much sleep over Obama's statements. They, and we, have heard such grand pronouncements before. Remember Jimmy Carter's declaration of independence from foreign oil in 1979? It proved a farce of the highest order. Later, in confessing America's addiction to oil, George Bush Jnr. declared that the country would slash its oil imports from the Middle East by 75 per cent by 2025. Yet, on US official figures, these imports are likely to double. Obama's interest in renewable energy is admirable. But will he have the courage to take the one action that more than anything else could put substance into his statements — increase the domestic tax take on fuel?

The Obama administration's approach to the Israeli– Palestinian conflict will show more clearly than anything the triumph of continuity over change. In 2007, Obama told the leading pro-Israeli lobby group, the America– Israel Public Affairs Committee (AIPAC), that a 'clear and strong commitment to the security of Israel' would always be 'my starting point'. America, he said, must preserve its 'total commitment to our unique defence relationship with Israel'. It must 'never seek to dictate what is best for Israelis and their security interests'. Given his audience on the occasion, it was understandable, perhaps, that Obama's speech contained not a single reference to illegal Israel settlements. But the trotting out of the mantras of there being no 'true Palestinian partner for peace', of the need to strengthen the hands of Palestinian 'moderates', and of maintaining the isolation of Hamas, showed unmistakably how much Obama is locked into a mindset that offers anything but fresh ideas for resolving the world's most intractable conflict.

Perhaps we should see this in the context of the contest for the presidency and Obama's concern not to frighten away Jewish voters—concerned perhaps by Obama's middle name (Hussein) or the Islamic currents of his early years in Indonesia. It is surely a sad indictment of the nature of American politics that its new president had to go out of his way to deny ever having been a Muslim. Why should this be of any greater concern than the strongly Jewish and pro-Israeli pedigree of Obama's subsequent choice for White House chief of staff, Rahm Israel Emmanuel? Among Emmanuel's various claims to fame is the fact that, as a US congressman, he accused the Bush administration of being too tough on Israel. If Obama really wants to change the Middle East, one of the first things he might have to do is change his chief of staff.

With Obama's vice-president, the signs are equally gloomy. Joseph Biden is on record as having 'never wavered from the notion' that the only time progress has been made in the Middle East is when the Arab world knows that there is 'no daylight' between the US and Israel. The Democrats' support for Israel, he suggested, 'comes from our gut, moves through our heart and ends up in our head'. But a bit of daylight—a bit of dictating—is sorely needed. Why can't the Obama administration drive home the fact that Israeli settlements threaten the long-term security of the Jewish state, that settling Jews on Palestinian territory presages an eventual single state solution in which Jews are a minority?

By acts of both commission and omission, Israel has helped to fracture Palestinian society and politics. That fracture can easily be trotted out as an excuse for inaction on the peace front. Can anyone seriously argue that Israel's long-term security is best secured by a deal with 'tame' Palestinians in the West Bank that leaves the Gaza Strip locked up and festering? Why can't Obama frame Israel's security in the only context that can help it in the long-term—that the US is committed to a genuine two-state solution encompassing pre-1967 Israel, the West Bank, and the Gaza Strip? This would involve major compromises by both sides, notably settlements and the security wall on the Israeli side, and the 'right of return' on the Palestinian. Certainly, the US should remain committed to ensuring Israel's security.

But it should stop giving Israel a blank cheque. A reality check is long overdue.

In trying to distance himself from the Bush administration over Iran, Obama promised the potentially oxymoronic path of 'aggressive diplomacy'. The problem for the US is that being tough on Iranian nuclear weapons ambitions carries with it a breathless hypocrisy. Whatever we think about those ambitions, Iran has joined, not initiated, the regional arms race. The US sticks with an umbilical relationship with nuclear-armed Israel, a cordial relationship with nuclear-armed India, and a tough-love relationship with nuclear-armed Pakistan. Iranian presidential elections, due in mid-2009, might see the end of Ahmadinejad. They are most unlikely to see the end of Iranian nuclear weapons ambitions. A more nuanced US approach to the Israeli–Palestinian conflict would have the potential benefits of undermining Iran's capacity to meddle in Palestinian, Lebanese, and Syrian affairs, and would also give the US greater negotiating coinage with Iran. We should not hold our breath.

In four year's time, the world will review the impact of America's first-ever non-white president. When it comes to the Middle East, the tragedy may well be that the only thing that truly changed was skin colour.

Acknowledgments, Sources, and Further Reading

The literature on the Middle East is vast. This is hardly surprising. The region's impact on our past, our present, and our future is profound. Daily, scores of opinions do battle about the region's seemingly intractable problems. Many of these opinions are well-researched and thoughtful. Some are not, with their ignorance and prejudices worn as a badge of honour.

In writing *Arabian Plights*, I have tapped the views of many whose knowledge of the region is greater than my own. I have tried as much as possible to acknowledge the work and ideas of others in the actual text of the book, rather than setting them out in lengthy endnotes. Listed below is a variety of sources that anyone with an interest in the Middle East will find useful, irrespective of whether they agree with the views on offer.

My reliance on some of these sources is self-evident. I also wish to thank three people in particular, whose help and hospitality enabled me to explore the ideas of others first-hand. They are two former colleagues in the Australian foreign service, Greg Moriarty and Robert Bowker, in their respective roles as the Australian ambassadors to Iran and Egypt, and my brother, David, a long-standing resident of the UAE. Needless to say, I bear sole responsibility for how I have presented all the material here.

The following does not capture every source mentioned in *Arabian Plights*, but it provides a guide to further reading, including the often-valuable material available in magazines and through Internet sites.

Books

Fouad Ajami, *The Arab Predicament: Arab political thought and practice since 1967*, Canto, 1992

——*The Foreigner's Gift: the Americans, the Arabs and the Iraqis in Iraq*, Free Press, 2006

Robert Baer, *Sleeping With the Devil: how Washington sold our soul for Saudi crude*, Crown, 2003

Antony Cordesman, *Saudi Arabia Enters the Twenty-First Century: the military and international security dimensions*, Praeger, 2003 (Much of Cordesman's valuable work can also be accessed through the Centre for Strategic and International Studies, Washington; see Internet sites below.)

Peter Demant, *Islam vs. Islamism: the dilemma of the Muslim world*, Praeger, 2006

Alan Dershowitz, *The Case for Israel*, John Wiley & Sons, 2003

Gwynne Dyer, *The Mess they Made: the Middle East after Iraq*, Scribe, 2007

Greg Fealy and Virginia Hooker (editors and compilers), *Voices of Islam in Southeast Asia: a contemporary sourcebook*, Institute of Southeast Asian Studies, Singapore, 2006

Fred Halliday, *Two Hours that Shook the World – September 11, 2001: causes and consequences*, Saqi, 2002

——*The Middle East in International Relations: power, politics and ideology*, Cambridge University Press, 2005

——*100 Myths About the Middle East*, Saqi, 2005

Hilal Khashan, *Arabs at the Crossroads: political identity and nationalism*, University Press of Florida, 2000

Samir Kasir, *Being Arab*, Verso 2006

Michael Klare, *Blood and Oil*, Penguin, 2004

Jeremy Leggett, *Half Gone: oil, gas, hot air and the global energy crisis*, Portobello, 2005

Bernard Lewis, *What Went Wrong?: Western impact and Middle Eastern responses*, Oxford University Press, 2002

——*The Crisis of Islam: holy war and unholy terror*, Phoenix, 2005

Vali Nasr, *The Shia Revival: how conflicts within Islam will shape the future*, Norton, 2006

Robert Pape, *Dying to Win: the strategic logic of suicide terrorism*, Scribe, 2005

Barry Rubin, *The Long War for Freedom: the Arab struggle for democracy in the Middle East*, John Wiley & Sons, 2006

Ian Rutledge, *Addicted to Oil: America's relentless drive for energy security*, I B Taurus, 2005

Matthew Simmons, *Twilight in the Desert: the coming Saudi oil shock and the world economy*, John Wiley & Sons, 2005

Robin Wright, Dreams and Shadows: the future of the Middle East, The Penguin Press, 2008

Magazines/journals

The Economist, London

The New York Review of Books, New York

Journal of Palestine Studies, Institute of Palestine Studies, University of California Press

Foreign Affairs, Council of Foreign Relations, New York

Internet sites

Arab Human Development Reports; www.arabhdr.org

Carnegie Endowment for International Peace; www.cargenieendowment.org

Centre for Strategic and International Studies, Washington, D.C.; www.csis.org

Chatham House/Royal Institute of International Affairs; www.chathamhouse.org.uk

Foundation for Middle East Peace (*Report on Israeli Settlement in the Occupied Territories*); *www.fmep.org*

Institute for the Analysis of Global Security; www.iags.org

International Crisis Group; www.crisisgroup.org

International Energy Agency; www.iea.org

International Monetary Fund; www.imf.org

Middle East Quarterly; www.meforum.org

Open Democracy; www.opendemocracy.net

Pew Global Attitudes Project; www.pewglobal.org

Saudi–US Relations Information Service (SUSRIS); www. saudi-us-relations.org

Stockholm International Peace Research Institute (SIPRI); www.sipri.org

US Congressional Committee on Foreign Affairs; www. internationalrelations.house.gov

US Department of Energy; www.energy.gov

US Department of State; www.state.gov

US Library of Congress, Congressional Research Service; www.loc.gov

US National Intelligence Council; www.dni.gov/nic

World Bank (see in particular *Economic Developments and Prospects, 2007; The Road Not Traveled: education reform in the Middle East and North Africa*); www.worldbank.org

Zogby International; www.zogby.com

Index